Praise for G.C. Dilsaver's Previous Work *

Kenneth Baker, S.J., the editor of the venerable *Homiletic & Pastoral Review* examined both Conrad Baars' work *Affirmation Psychotherapy* (which is often touted as the Thomistic or Catholic Psychotherapy) and G.C. Dilsaver's work *Imago Dei Psychotherapy*. In doing so, Baker found that *Imago Dei Psychotherapy* is "an invaluable tool" "fully in accord" with Thomistic principles, but had "some doubts" about the validity of Baars' *Affirmation Therapy* as a Thomistic integration.

Baker writes in regards to Baars' seminal work *Affirmation Psychotherapy*, "We find in the book an attempted wedding between some of the insights of psychology and the philosophy of St. Thomas Aquinas.... Baars claims that St. Thomas agrees with him. I have some doubts about that; there are some important distinctions that should be made about the emotions, and our author does not make them. I attribute that to the fact that he is a psychologist and not a philosopher." **

Conversely, in examining Dilsaver's *Imago Dei Psychotherapy*, Baker proclaims that "In this treatise on clinical psychology, we find a current presentation which is fully in accord with traditional scholastic philosophy and theology. The whole Catholic worldview of man made in the image of God, a composite being of spirit and matter, is the philosophical basis of *Imago Dei Psychotherapy*. This is an invaluable tool for Catholic counselors, psychologists and psychiatrists whose goal it is to bring their therapants to a state of mental health which is in accord with both the natural law and divine revelation."

~~~~

"Dr. Dilsaver is rightly considered by many the father of Christian psychology, for his book *Imago Dei Psychotherapy* enunciated the foundational principles of the first fully integrated Christian psychotherapeutic conceptualization." ***

Catholic University of America

~~~~

This book proffers a **powerful antidote** to a purely secular form of psychology: a fully integrated Catholic psychotherapeutic conceptualization.

John O'Connell (Editor of Fr. John Hardon's *Catholic Faith Magazine*)

~~~~

I have just been reading a fascinating book: *Imago Dei Psychotherapy: A Catholic Conceptualization* by G.C. Dilsaver, an American Catholic psychologist. It is about healing those who are mentally ill because of depression, borderline personality disorders and so on, by helping to restore the "image of God" within them....

London's Catholic Herald, Francis Phillips

---

* N.B., that the unique discipline of psychomoralitics goes far beyond the groundbreaking seminal work of *Imago Dei Psychotherapy*. Unlike *Imago Dei Psychotherapy*, *Psychomoralitics* is purified of all erroneous, obfuscating, and reductionistic elements inherent in the mental health conceptualization; and thus enabled to be a fully developed Thomistic conceptualization, strikingly and diametrically opposed to the mental health conceptualization.

** Baker, Kenneth, *Homiletic & Pastoral Review*, August/September 2008.

*** Catholic University of America Press Release
https://web.archive.org/web/20131203134340/http://cuapress.cua.edu/books/viewb ook.cfm? book=XDID

PSYCHOMORALITICS

PsychoMoralitics
The Soul-Deep Alternative
to the Failed Mental Health Professions

G.C. Dilsaver, P/M, PsyD, MTS

Imago Dei Press

ISBN# 978-0-9993607-1-2

IMAGO DEI PRESS
WWW.IMAGODEIPRESS.COM

To her, who in immaculate receptivity to Absolute Reality,
magnified that Reality in perfect fulfillment of the human vocation.

CONTENTS

NOTA BENE

DSM Psychomoralitics is a **NON-DSM** Discipline. DSM disciplines and practices are those that follow the scientifically invalid and intra-professionally repudiated *Diagnostic & Statistical Manual*, which is the foundational document of the Mental Health System.

As a definitively NON-DSM and non-mental health discipline and practice, psychomoralitics does not utilize, employ, or implement in any manner or form the DSM and/or mental health conceptualizations, nosologies, terminologies, or treatments. In addition, Psychomoralitics is not compromised by the degrading privacy invasive requirements of the Mental Health System.

The following manuscript presents the thoroughly developed and systematized science of psychomoralitics. Psychomoralitics is a unique scientific discipline, and by definition not located upon the same continuum as that of the mental health professions. The psychomoralitic continuum is that of the deepest and most essential human well-being and flourishing, whereas the mental health continuum is that of superficial and gross manifestation of symptomatic mentation and behavior. Thus the relationship between psychomoralitics and mental health is unlike, for example,

i

alternative/homeopathic medicine and mainstream/allopathic medicine, which are both upon the same medical continuum of physical health.

Herein, "mental health profession" and "mental health field" (a.k.a., behavioral health, etc.) refers to the entirety of mental health clinical practices, both the disciples and the specific professions, such as psychology, psychiatry, counseling, addiction treatment, etc. That is, the mental health field entails all activities that practice under the term "mental health," et al., which is statutorily defined and controlled in totality by the mental health system.

Herein, "mental health system" (aka, behavioral health, etc.) refers to the complex that controls all services, practices, and clinical disciplines that utilize the term "mental health," et al. This controlling entity is a multifaceted bureaucracy controlled by the State, and aligned with the insurance and pharmaceutical industries, and the mental health professions' regulatory and educational agencies.

Herein, unless otherwise stated, "psychology" and "psychologist" refers to psychotherapeutic clinical intervention, which the vast majority of psychologists are involved in. While psychology remains a valid science in regards to the measurement of empirical data, it goes beyond its competency in regards to philosophical anthropology and subsequently the humanistic clinical intervention it practices. This anthropological incompetency is most apparent and harmful in the mental health field's practice of psychotherapy and psychopharmacology.

Finally, this manuscript, though condemnatory of the mental health system, ***entails no criticism of those who are receiving mental health services.*** For the mental health system has been foisted upon the public by means of a saturating commercial, medical, and governmental propagandization; and those seeking relief, for what is in reality a psychomoral issue, have been made to believe that they have nowhere else to turn. Nor is it an indiscriminate condemnation of those delivering mental health services, for, it is assumed that most mental health practitioners, even if misguided, are nonetheless well intended and have even been able to accomplish some good for those in their care despite the deficiencies of their conceptualizations and the pernicious demands of their licensure.

THERE ARE SMALL MINDS WHO ASSERT

THAT IT IS BETTER TO BE A CONTENTED PIG

THAN AN UNHAPPY HUMAN BEING.

BUT HE WHO HAS ONCE TASTED

THE FLAVOR OF HUMANITY,

HE WILL—EVEN IN PROFOUND MISERY—

PREFER THE UNHAPPINESS OF MAN

TO THE CONTENTMENT OF THE PIG.

IT IS WELL, THEREFORE,

TO CAUSE DISQUIETUDE IN HUMAN SOULS

AND TO ENKINDLE IN THEM A MIGHTY YEARNING.

Miguel de Unamuno
(1864 - 1936)

PREFACE

ALL OF US, either ourselves, our family members, or our acquaintances, have received "diagnoses" and treatments from the mental health professions. Until now, and the advent of psychomoralitics, these professions were the only clinical option most people have had when dealing with serious psychomoral distress and its sometimes manifestation in disordered mental symptomology. This is because the mental health professions have been promoted, marketed, and subsidized to the hilt by the mental health system: a complex comprised of the State, the insurance and pharmaceutical industries, and their sanctioned mental health organizations. As a result, the mental health system and its professions have experienced an unprecedented exponential growth. Indeed, this juggernaut mental health system is nothing less than ubiquitous in today's culture, infiltrating everything from schools, to workplace, to churches, and even the sacrosanct realm of marriage and family.

But in spite of the unmatched financial success, growth, and dominance of the mental health professions, and though they occasionally and haphazardly accomplish good, they have conclusively been both a dismal failure and purveyor of harm.[1] As per my own education in clinical psychology, I can note that many of the best and brightest in the mental health professions

---

1   As has been widely noted in a plethora of critiques both from within the mental health professions and without. See Appendix C: *Intra-Professional Condemnations*. p.237

will at some time during their training despair of their
discipline's efficacy. Some quit, and the best usually early on. But
so too, many push doubts aside and allow themselves to get
carried away by the treadmill of the mental health system,
impelled by their own understandable desire for survival and
success.

From the very beginning of my doctoral training, I too
despaired of the efficacy of the mental health disciplines. But
unlike most of my erstwhile colleagues, who for the most part
went straight from an undergraduate major in psychology to
graduate psychology, I serendipitously brought to my study a
degree in philosophy and an advanced degree in theology, as well
as an undergraduate education in the liberal arts and the Great
Books of Western Civilization (plus two stints in the U.S. Marine
Corps and ample life experience). The result being that I was able
to *doubly despair,* not only seeing the hapless and ineffectual
results of the mental health professions, but seeing as well the
gravely deficient, and at times manifestly absurd, philosophical
understanding of the human person found in the various personality
theories, psychotherapies, and overall conceptualizations embedded
in the mental health system.

But unlike those who, in the face of the evermore apparent
quasi-quackery of the mental health professions, either quit or
successfully denied and blindly coped with it, I was blessed with
a third alternative. I was afforded nothing less than a vision; no, not
a mystical vision, but a vision glorious and amazing nonetheless. It
was a vision in black and white, letters upon paper.[2] It was a vision

---

2 Special note must be given to Josef Pieper's (1904—1997) *Living the Truth*
   (Ignatius Press; Reprint edition; November 1, 1989), which being read while
   moonlighting as a substitute teacher during an especially non-interactive
   high school class, produced the proverbial "ah-ha" moment.

afforded by the world's most venerable philosophical understanding of the human person. So, providentially, from the beginning of my training I was able to vet my studies, and concurrently develop a conceptualization and practice according to the supremely validated and perennial philosophical anthropology of Western scholasticism; a scholasticism that finds its fullest expression in Thomism. Yet this conceptualization and practice, this *psychomoralitics*, with its timeless foundation and animating spirit, was nothing less than *diametrically opposed* to the conceptualization and practice—and yes, the animating spirit as well—of the mental health system.

So I worked undercover. While jumping through the hoops of an American Psychological Association doctoral program and hospital internship, and the subsequent training and examinations required for my licensing in many states, I continued to practice and develop psychomoralitics as per my duty to my therapants and to truth itself. During this time I produced scholarly works that presented psychomoralitics[3] in a manner that I hoped would be somewhat palatable to the mental health system, so as to colonize, if not altogether reform, that system. But this attempt necessarily entailed compromise. Yes, psychomoralitics is psychology, but a true *psychology* that is actually *"the study of the soul."* But psychomoralitics was not *psychology* as implicitly understood by the mental health system, a system that does not in fact or practice, even recognize the soul.

---

3 Invited Presentation at American Psychological Association Division 36 Psychology of Religion, Mid-Year Meeting Baltimore, MD; *Secularity as a Metaphysical Placeholder to Ensure Scientific Integrity and Foster Worldview Diversity in Clinical Psychology* (February 2003). Invited Presentation at American Psychological Association National Convention, Washington, D.C.; *A Thomistic Psychotherapeutic Conceptualization* (August 2007).

In the course of over a decade of psychomoralitic development and treatment it became undeniably and increasingly clear that the mental health system was not only utterly irreformable, but utterly corrupt as well. The mental health system is utterly irreformable because it has too much at stake in its dual agenda of advancing both a reductionistic dehumanizing anthropology and its political and financial bureaucratic power. Though hid under the false cover of benignity, this synergistic dual agenda of dehumanization and power comprises the mental health system's very *raison d'etat*.

The mental health system's reductionistic focus on mere manifestations of mentations or behaviors (thus the designation as "mental" or "behavioral" health) in effect eliminates that which transcends that symptomology. This reductionism eliminates not only that which psychomoralitics advances to be the cause of mal-being,[4] ego-reactivity, and much disordered mental or behavioral symptomology, but renders obsolete the very essence of the human person. By reducing the person down to mere symptoms of mentation or behavior the mental health system renders that person non-transcendent, without sacrosanct and unfathomable depths, and thus a mere quantifiable entity that is confined within a false and brutalizing paradigm. In effect, the mental health paradigm renders the person manipulable, controllable, and ultimately enslavable. This has never been acceptable to me, nor to any other psychomoralitic practitioners; but nor should it be to anyone who claims to be a *healer of the soul*. Indeed, the ethical and moral obligations adhered to in psychomoralitics, and other healing disciplines, has been set in stone since time immemorial:

---

4   The psychomoral continuum goes from mal-being to well-being, with ego-reactivity and coping in-between.

"I will follow that system of regimen which, according to my ability and judgment, I consider for the benefit of my patients, and abstain from whatever is deleterious and mischievous."

(Hippocratic Oath, 500 BC)

Intrinsic to the false and harmful mental health system's reductionistic conceptualization is a susceptibility to corruption. Ideas have consequences, and consequentially the mental health system has become corrupt to the core. The mental health system's rapid acquirement of bureaucratic power has shockingly resulted in its gaining of a total and violent coercive control[5] over its professions, practitioners, and patients. In this the mental health system presents a prime example of a State and corporate empowered bureaucratic agency becoming fully weaponized against its very constituency.

---

5 There are two glaring manifestations of the mental health system as a deep state bureaucracy fully weaponized against its patients. The first is evidenced in the mental health system having its very own Orwellian "mental health courts." These extra-judiciary, unconstitutional, and unaccountable mental health courts often sentence the convicted to a life-long psychotropic drugging. Such a sentencing is indeed a death sentence, if not immediately to the body, at least to the possible human flourishing of the condemned. The second manifestation of deep State mental health malfeasance is the requirement that licensed mental health practitioners archive all records and notes ever taken in sessions, and be ready and willing to turned these over for any reason and at any time when so ordered by the State, courts, licensing boards, or upon request by anyone who is litigating against a patient—*even if contrary to a patient's wishes or harmful to his good*. While the mental health system falsely advances that there are safeguards on patient records (e.g., the myriad of hapless, window-dressing HIPPA regulations), the shocking truth is that there is *zero confidentiality* guaranteed to those engaged in any mental health services; a supremely sordid fact intentionally kept camouflaged by the mental health system.

The mental health system's false theoretical conceptualization and ensuing perverse ethos is now inextricably wed to an unbridled bureaucratic power. The mental health system has thus been rendered antithetical not only to psychomoralitics, but to the timeless *noblesse oblige* inherent in the sacrosanct duties a healer of the soul incurs in regards to the well-being and protection of those in his care. The thorough and irredeemable corruption of the mental health system (made salient in its unconscionably—but adamantly rejected—demands that my own practice be weaponized against my therapants), coupled with the full scientific development of psychomoralitics (with its proven and superlative efficacy[6]), finally deemed it no longer ethically or clinically acceptable for the practice of psychomoralitics to be obfuscated under, nor even tacitly compliant to, the malignant gargantuan that is the mental health system.

As will be enunciated, the mental health system and its professions are a major cause of essential mal-being, ego-reactivity, and the enslavement of the human spirit, and thus in the long run, only exacerbate even the symptomatic mental disordering they purportedly treat. But in this, not only is psychomoralitics a separate discipline diametrically opposed conceptually to the mental health disciplines, but fortuitously it is the very *anti-discipline*—or more aptly the *anti-dotal* discipline—that remedies the iatrogenic ills caused by the mental health system and its professions.

Finally, note well that psychomoralitics (and herein is the source of its validity and efficacy) is strikingly *not* the work of any one person. Thus, I must render thanks to those that have collaborated in, and journeyed with me, in the formulation of

6 For qualitative results see http://www.psychomoral.com/testimonies. Further quantified results of efficacy will follow as per the degree and variation of promulgation.

psychomoralitics. Firstly, I thank the giants of perennial Western thought, as well as those subsequent scholarly keepers and renewers of that thought, who have provided psychomoralitics with its patrimony of philosophical and anthropological principles. Secondly, I thank those who have and are training with me as mentors and psychomoralists (all taken, not from the ranks of college psyche majors with good grades, but from the grounded and proven ranks[7] of life); may their expertise and efficacy exceed mine. Thirdly, and most heartfelt, I thank the therapants that have graced my practice and provided such an edifying example of courageous openness to the unfathomable spectrum of reality, both in its piecing sorrows and sublime joys. May this openness to the fullness of human existence—and the psychomoral freedom, peace, and flourishing it engenders—be as well the fruit of these ensuing pages.

G.C. Dilsaver, M/P, PsyD, MTS

Institute of Psychomoralitics

12 December 2017

Fiesta de la Virgen de Guadalupe

---

7   See Appendix F: *Training and Certification in Psychomoralitics.* p.255

1. The Ancient Applied Anew

PSYCHOMORALITICS IS THE INTERVENTIVE SCIENCE OF THE SOUL. Strictly speaking then, the psychomoralitic could be considered akin to the *psychologic* or *psychiatric* in their literal meaning as "of the science of the soul" and "of the healing of the soul." However, the terms *psychology* and *psychiatry*, and their derivations, have been co-opted, are indeed statutorily owned, by the mental health system. Yet the mental health system that owns the terminology of the science and treatment of the psyche/soul does not recognize the existence of the psyche/soul. So a new terminology free from the mental health system's etymological evisceration, false parameters, and coercive controls, and fully in accord with the authentic meaning of the science and treatment of the soul was needed. Hence the advent of the term *psychomoralitic*, and its root term *psychomoral* for the realm it treats.

It is from the psyche or soul that comes the power or ability to be moral. *Moral* means an act that involves the rational assent to truth and the volitional choosing or loving of that truth as the good. Thus it is within the psychomoral realm that resides the specific difference of the human person. It is within this essential human realm that the soul-deep science of psychomoralitics

1

intervenes to rectify mal-being and ego-reactivity, and to effect essential well-being, innermost peace, and human flourishing.

The mental health professions' failure to efficaciously treat even its designated "mental and behavioral disorders," is due to its nonrecognition of the human person's essential psychomoral realm. Indeed, most of the mental or behavioral symptomology, the so-called mental disorders or illnesses, have their origins in the psychomoral realm and are but symptomatic manifestations of mal-being in that realm. The mental health field's deficiency in understanding the essential psychomoral nature of the human person has resulted not only in failure but in grave iatrogenic mistreatment that exacerbates and accelerates psychomoral mal-being, and as a result the superficial mental/behavioral symptomatic disordering.

Due in part to the mental health professions' erroneous conceptualizations and subsequent mistreatments, psychomoral mal-being has reached pandemic proportions in post-modern technologically developed countries, and especially the West. For statistical evidence of this psychomoral mal-being pandemic, today's tragic suicide rate among young adults can be taken as concisely indicative. Not only does such a youth based statistic rule out the confounding variables associated with the current increased longevity, but so too suicide is seen both traditionally and clinically as the most severe and culminating manifestation of psychological disordering. As such, the catastrophic increase in severity and frequency of psychological disordering is statistically demonstrated in the fact that *the suicide rate among young adults rose three-fold between 1950 and 1990, and continues to rise.[8]*

The Technarcistic West

Like the physiological black plague of bacteremia that once devastated the late medieval West, a psychomoral black plague now devastates the post-modern technological West and its milieu. Contemporary Western man has increasingly distanced himself from his philosophical and ethical roots, as well as from the natural law in which these roots find their moorings. This is made possible to an unprecedented degree by the rise of technology and the ensuing artificial habitat that facilitates the denial of (though not escape from) basic truths of human nature, existence and reality. The result is the advent of today's *Technarcistic Man.*[9]

The psychomorally devolved and malformed technarcistic person is cut off from his ancient cultural moorings, natural law, and even common sense, having ample means to anesthetize himself to reality. The pathogenesis of this disconnect and anesthetization is an increased unawareness and blindness that progresses upon a continuum where the technarcistic person becomes myopically and egoistically fixated on himself and his

8 In 21 of the 30 countries in the World Health Organization (WHO) European region, suicide rates in males aged 15-19 rose between 1979 and 1996. http://www.nber.org/chapters/c10690.pdf

9 See Appendix B: *Technarcistic Man.* p.233

subjective good and progressively less open to objective reality, truth, and good. Such a myopic fixation has resulted in the 21st Century West's pandemic of psychomoral mal-being.

Seeking the remedy for the contemporary West's pandemic of psychomoral mal-being reasonably begins with an examination of the circumstances, ethoses, and resources of that culture itself. This entails as well an examination of the ancient matrix from which the contemporary West sprang. It is also at least probable to expect, and it is herein advanced, that it is in the ancient and perennial wisdom of Western civilization that the remedy for its current plague of psychomoral mal-being is to be found. Indeed, the perennial wisdom of the West readily provides an integral philosophical anthropology that integrates both a psychological and moral understanding of the nature of the human person, as well as a commonsensical philosophy of existence and reality.

It is furthermore advanced herein that not only is the cure of psychomoral mal-being to be found in the perennial philosophical anthropology of the West, but that the very rejection of, and alienation from, this perennial Western understanding of human nature is at the basis of the technarcistic West's pandemic of psychomoral mal-being. Strikingly, the Western mental health field has from its inception rejected, and over time only become quite hostile to, this perennial anthropology. As will be seen in subsequent chapters, this rejection and hostility has in fact rendered the mental health field a major facilitator of psychomoral mal-being and, counterproductively, the mental symptomology it formally seeks to alleviate.

A Radically New Discipline

The unique soul-deep science of psychomoralitics is truly the ancient applied anew, for it is based upon the timeless philosophical anthropology that is foundational and perennial to the West—but even to the East[10] and thus the world.[11] Even before discussing its unprecedented validity, it can be said without controversy that within perennial Western philosophy is found the most venerable, expostulated, and enduring conceptualization of the human person in his specific difference.[12] This key perennial philosophical anthropology upon which psychomoralitics is based was present at the birth of Western civilization in ancient Greece, was fully developed under the auspices of the Western philosophical scholasticism, and found its most concise

---

10 Aristotelian thought was fundamental for the great Eastern Arabic philosophers Abu 'Ali al-Husayn ibn Sina (980—1037) and Abū l-Walīd Muḥammad Ibn'Aḥmad Ibn Rušd (1126–-1198) better known in the West respectively as Avicenna and Averroes.

11 The Thomistic synthesis was achieved with its namesake's writings, yet has continued a vibrant development and application throughout the centuries. The last truly explosive renewal of Thomistic scholarship coincided with and indeed hastened the advent of experimental and clinical psychology.

12 Thus the psychomoralitic conceptualization derives from an inherited patrimony.

expression in Thomism.[13] It was strongly resurgent throughout
the 20th century, and remains so today. This anthropology's
academics of philosophical scholasticism are the same academics
that ushered in the empirical sciences.

The anthropology of scholastic Thomism scientifically defines
the rational/volitional realm (herein termed the psychomoral
realm) and holds this realm to be the essence and specific
difference of the human person. Psychomoralitics is unique
because it is the first topographical conceptualization of this
perennial, indeed universal and commonsensically, Thomistic
understanding of the human person. It is this unique
psychomoralitic topography that allows it to be readily applied to
the person in the advancement of psychomoral well-being and in
the remedying of mal-being.

The new discipline of psychomoralitics differs fundamentally
from the various disciplines of the status quo mental health
system. It is psychomoralitics' very radicality and ancient
newness that, at very least, proffers the hope that its interventions
may be truly efficacious, whereas more of the same from the
mental health field does not. Psychomoralitics is radical both
because it goes back to the *root* (Lt., *radix*) Western understanding
of essential human anthropology, and because it is radical in
being diametrically opposed conceptually and in its clinical

13 St. Thomas Aquinas (1225 – 7 March 1274) is the father of Thomism. All
of modern Western philosophy can be said to take its bearings from his
works, either as a development thereof or as an opposition thereto.

dynamics to the mental/behavioral health disciplines. The discipline of psychomoralitics differs fundamentally from the disciplines of the mental health field, for the very goals differ. While psychomoralitics seeks to promote essential well-being and remedy psychomoral mal-being, thus treating actual etiology, the goal of the mental health field is the mere alleviation of superficial mental symptomology, a goal that most often does harm to the psychomoral realm. In fact, the discipline of psychomoralitics is diametrically opposed to the mental health disciplines because—both in intent and in practice, both in goals and thus applications and interventions—these disciplines work *against* each other. In sum, and as will be seen, that which the mental health disciplines seek to facilitate, psychomoralitics seeks to abnegate.

As will be elaborated upon, the discipline of psychomoralitics and the mental health disciplines have a distant common impetus in philosophical and experimental psychology, but the mental health disciplines upon inception deviated from the origins of that impetus; indicating why psychomoralitics is not an alternative mental health discipline but rather a unique discipline of essential human well-being. The discipline of psychomoralitics differs qualitatively from the mere symptomological, and thus reductionistic and superficial, conceptualizations and treatments found in the mental health disciplines and strikes at the very psychological/moral root of all psychomoral mal-being and essential human mal-being itself. As such, psychomoralitics as a discipline is not in any way—ideologically, definitively, clinically, or statutorily—subsumed under the mental health disciplines.

The Psychomoral Realm

While psychomoralitics' attributing of the causative dynamics of disordered mental symptomology to an underlying interior realm of the human person is not unique, its locating and descriptive demarcation of, and subsequent intervention within, the anthropological topography of this incorporeal psychomoral realm is. From this psychomoralitic topography, based on the perennial and commonsensical understanding of the nature of the human person, comes as well the concept of essential well-being and mal-being, which stands starkly against the reductionistic mental health field's concept of symptomatic mentation and behavior.

Again, the term "psychomoral" is composed of *psyche* and *moral*. Psyche refers to the essence of the human person that consists of the rational volitional soul. Moral refers to the specific human functioning of that soul in its receiving-the-real, assenting-to-truth, and choosing-the-good.[14] The psychomoral realm then entails both the deliberate act, the indeliberate act, and those acts appearing indistinguishably in-between. The

---

14 *Receiving-the-real, assenting-to-truth, and choosing-the-good* rightly and without impediment determines the degree of psychomoral/essential well-being. See Chapter 4: *Reality-Based Conceptualization.* p.63

indeliberate act in itself does not involve full freedom and hence moral culpability, thus not all that which emanates from the psychomoral realm is strictly speaking a "moral act." The free moral act is the human *qua* human act.

The human person can perform a moral act because he is capable of consciously assenting to truth and volitionally choosing it as a good or rejecting it for a lower good. But a person's ability to assent to the truth or choose the good can be impeded by established psychomoral mal-being, namely coping mechanisms and dominating ego passions, that hamper assent and choice. It is the diminishment of these mechanisms and passions, and the subsequent freeing of the reason and will, that is the goal of the psychomoralitic process. So while the choice made in a moral act can be objectively right or wrong, a person is not always fully free in the choosing and thus is not always fully culpable for the wrong choice.

It is in the moral or fully psychomoral act, the *rational assent to truth,* and *volitional choosing of the good,* that is found the specific difference that distinguishes the human person from animals. This moral ability that is the specific difference of the human is also the key to psychomoral well-being. For when a person assents to the fullest truth and chooses the most integral good, a person is assenting to and choosing reality; and what more is essential human well-being than living in accord with reality?

The psychomoral realm is where character and personality, reason and volition, choice and love, virtue and vice resides. The psychomoral realm is where reason and volition, that is, assent to truth and decisions to love, interplay. The psychomoral realm is where the drama of the truly human takes place. The psychomoral realm is the intangible but essential variable of the human person. The psychomoral realm consists of that which informs the intellect/mind with its unique powers of reason and volition. The psychomoral realm entails deeper still elements that are immeasurable because immaterial, that is, it entails the fathomless soul.

No matter how one would specifically define this soul, it must nonetheless necessarily be defined at least as an immeasurable and intangible essential force in the thought, passion, and behavior of an individual. Whatever the soul is, it is nonetheless where the unfathomable and mysterious depths of the human person resides. The soul is also then that which makes a person more than his measurable and quantifiable—that is physiological—aspects, and thus makes the person a being that transcends any material coercion.

Psychomoral Mal-Being vs. Mental Disorder

Psychomoralitics promotes essential human well-being and treats the root of psychomoral mal-being within the realm of the specific or essential human difference that is man's rational/volitional ability. Again, note well that psychomoralitics has a different objective than that of the mental/behavioral health disciplines which, as their name indicates, treat superficial mental or behavioral symptomatic disordering. Note too, that psychomoralitics as a discipline of the soul is an unabashedly spiritual discipline, whereas the mental health system eschews the spiritual. Psychomoralitics, as it were, puts the *soul* back into *psych*ology, by reclaiming and reinstating that "study of the soul."

Mental refers to mentation and *behavioral* refers to actions, as such both refer to end results or symptomology. Thus the mental health field treats resultant symptomology, but not the causes of this symptomology that are found in the deeper and deepest psychomoral realm of the soul. That which the mental health field studies and treats are, for the most part (save for the organic disorders it fails to distinguish), mere symptomatic mentations and behaviors.

It is the mental health field's superficial conceptualization based on symptomology that misdirects its efforts and treatment to the point of not only ineffectuality but of iatrogenic harm. This ineffectuality and "treatment induced" harm is due to the mental health field's unawareness of the essential psychomoral realm from which much of its designated symptomology has its origins. This unawareness, and subsequent mistreatment, by the mental health profession results in serious iatrogenic debilitation, trauma to the psychomoral realm, and often further exacerbation of the symptomology it seeks to alleviate.

Psychology: The *Supposed* Study of the Soul

Properly understood, a true clinical psychology (again read *psychomoralitics*) would not primarily be about material *gray matter*, but rather about a material/immaterial *gray area*. For the question will always remain: Where does the organic realm give way to the psychomoral realm? Traditionally and poetically in the West, the heart has been thought of as the seat of the soul, and in the poetic tradition of the East the soul is located in the abdomen. This is because it is in the heart and abdomen that the sympathetic nervous system is most felt in correspondence to cognitions and passions.

Scientifically, but still somewhat poetically, if there is one area that can be said to "house" the soul it is the brain. Even though the soul cannot literally be encompassed by matter, it is the life and organicity of the brain that specifically makes possible mortal human life, for man's specific difference from the other animals is his rationality. Some argue that once the brain is dead human life is impossible, that is, traditionally, the soul has departed. This argument advances that the lack of the minimal requisite neurological organicity (for example, in the case of a completely encephalitic infant), makes human life *qua* human apparently impossible; that is, human ensoulment may not be present because there is no possibility of the soul expressing its rationality. Others argue that human ensoulment does take place because the potentiality lies in the embryonic genetic make-up and embryonic teleology of the infant, regardless of the physical defect.[15]

The powers of the psyche, even though non-material, still require organicity for their actualization; that is, the powers of the soul require the means of the brain to express themselves and thus be discernible. A remarkable example of this psyche/brain relation can be found in the *autistic savant syndrome*. Here, individuals with severe organic neurological impairment may display the rarest of genius in certain areas. An autistic savant, though having a global intelligence quotient that is in the range of mental retardation, may nonetheless have, for instance, the ability to instantaneously perform complex mathematical calculations, or may have perfect musical performance recall. Such displays of intelligence may surpass the abilities of even those in the designated field (e.g., mathematics or music) who are of the highest genius level.

In this autistic savant phenomenon, it appears that the powers of the soul—themselves undiminished but frustrated by organic deficiency—can be channeled, concentrated, and manifested via remaining avenues of intact organicity. This phenomenon of the autistic savant syndrome appears to be a

---

15 Philosophically, it seems that the latter position is the correct one since partial diminishment of neurological function does not diminish the humanity of the impaired, nor does the absence of a physical possibility impact spiritual potential. Ethically, that is, when deciding whether or not a neurologically deficient person has the right to life, acceptance of the latter principle is mandatory.

startling example of the non-material nature of *prime intelligence*.[16] For in observing this channeling of intelligence there is a demonstrable fluidity to that intelligence. This fluidity does not find its origins in organicity, physiology, or even chemical conductivity. It is a fluidity more fluid than liquid itself; it is the fluidity of the spiritual powers of the soul/psyche.[17]

No matter how advanced neuro-imagery or other diagnostic tests become there can never be a picture produced, or a blood test or neurochemical analyzed, that will indicate that one has one of the so-called mental disorders, such as depression, bipolarism, obsessive compulsivity, or schizophrenia. This is because the so-called mental disorders are but a mere categorization of symptoms and thus have not within themselves their own cause. Nor is their cause even within the realm of physicality. Rather the basis of disordered mental symptomology is in the immaterial psychomoral realm of the person, and a picture or a sample of the immaterial cannot be taken.

---

16 *Prime intelligence* is here used as in *prime* in *prime matter*. As per the scholastic definition, prime matter is the fundamental, potential principle of all bodily substances.

17 "It is not so much the definitiveness of perception but rather the breadth and depth of perception, the full experiential range of human existence from the tragic to the triumphant, that is the hallmark of mental health. Indeed, it is axiomatic that those who lack some degree of openness to empirical sensation or intellectual processing because of organic deficiency seem more fully open to transcendent realities, and to God Himself, and thus manifest a sort of autistic-mystic-savant syndrome." G.C. Dilsaver, *Imago Dei Psychotherapy*, Chapter 6, § *Openness-to-Reality*, pg. 88, *Sapientia Press*, 2008.

The presence of an immaterial psychomoral realm does not mean that physiology is not necessary for the operation of the human mind, nor that physiology does not impact psychomoral well-being. But the presence of the psychomoral realm does mean that the human person cannot be reduced down to his merely quantifiable parts. Thus the presence and acknowledgment of the psychomoral also means that the human person has an unfathomable and transcendent inner mystery that is to be revered.

2. THE FAILED & DANGEROUS MENTAL HEALTH SYSTEM

A primary purpose of [the DSM-V research agenda] was to determine why progress has been so limited and to offer strategic insights that may lead to a more etiologically-based diagnostic system. The group ultimately concluded that given the current state of technological limitations, the field is years, and possibly decades, away from having a fully explicated etiology, and patho-physiology, based classification system for psychiatry.

—Michael B. First, M.D.[18] Editor of DSM-IV-TR

PSYCHOMORALITICS HAS BEEN DEVELOPED out of clinical necessity, a necessity arising from the mental health field's lack of efficacy in the curing of maladies of essential human mal-being; and indeed out of the mental health field's own iatrogenic[19] acceleration of this psychomoral mal-being. This failure and harm is true both of psychotherapies and psychotropics, both of

---

18 *A Research Agenda for DSM-V: Summary of the DSM-V Preplanning White Papers*. Published in May 2002.

19 *Iatrogenic*: Treatment induced harm.

17

psychology and psychiatry. The point will not be belabored here for there are a plethora of studies and findings on the failure of the mental health profession issued from their very own ranks.[20]

Yet in spite of the mental health field's lack of therapeutic efficacy, the bulk of it's practitioners have been lulled into a coping[21] complacency. This coping complacency is understandable, for until now, and the advent of psychomoralitics, there has been no viable alternative. So too, the mental health field's lack of therapeutic efficacy has been endured by its intelligentsia—its professors, psychologists, and psychiatrists—who, though fully aware of its glaring failures, faithfully await an explication of so-called mental disorder in terms of a biological basis. This expected explication was at a revival pitch in the 1990s[22] with the improvements and inventions in electronic neuro-imaging that promised great new revelations. This expectation has been dashed, requiring the mental health field to issue declarations such as it is *"years, and possibly decades, away from having a fully explicated etiology, and patho-physiology, based classification system"* (see Chapter 2 prelude).

But still, hope springs eternal, and even many of the most prominent and authoritative critics of the main stream chemical imbalance theories rigidly refuse to look beyond the physiological: "Undoubtedly, there are neurobiological and genetic causes for all

---

20 See Appendix C: *Intra-Professional Condemnations.* p.237

21 Coping is not necessarily indicative of essential well-being.
    See Chapter 8: *Egoistic Coping.* p.139

22 The 1990's were proclaimed by presidential fiat to be "the decade of the brain."

mental disorders, but they are still beyond our understanding."[23] Why "undoubtedly"? Because the mental health field is but a sample of a dogmatically materialistic Western intelligentsia. The mental health "high-priests" preach that the human person is nothing but a material being, yet they must admit that there is no tangible material evidence as to the cause of mental disorder. This glaring lack of material evidence should in itself be an empirical clue: *the very empirical absence of material causes of symptomatic mental disordering suggests that the cause is not material or biological at all.*

Though revising the day and time of the great revelation of a fully, or even partially, explicated biologically based etiology and patho-physiology may give hope to the mental health field faithful, it is a false hope. It is herein advanced that regardless of any future advances in technology there will not be—and can never be—a great revelation as to the biological basis of symptomatic mental disordering. This is because symptomatic mental disorder is but a superficial manifestation of a non-tangible soul-deep etiology; that is, these symptoms are manifestations of mal-being that do not have a biological basis but rather a psychomoral one.

---

23 "Unfortunately we know a good bit less about what we are doing than you might think. When I find myself using phrases like 'chemical imbalance' and 'serotonin deficiency', it is usually because I'm trying to convince a reluctant patient to take a medication. Using these words makes their illness seem more biological, taking some of the stigma away." Daniel J. Carlat, M.D., Associate Clinical Professor of Psychiatry at *Tufts University School of Medicine.*

The Mental Health System

This dogmatic belief in the biological basis of mental disorder and its reductionistic view of the human person as soul-less, spirit-less, and non-transcendent, is not only the overriding academic orientation of the mental health field, its disciplines and professions, but a mandate enforced in the most real and practical terms on that field by the mental health system.

For all intents and purposes the mental health system (the all controlling bureaucratic power formed by the complex of the State, professional mental health organizations, and the insurance and pharmaceutical industries) has under it auspices the entirety of the mental health field. Even the theoretical aspects of the mental health disciplines, the academic contents and orientations of their schools and programs of certification, are controlled by the mental health system. For if these schools and programs are to actually to produce practicing mental health professionals there is a required State licensing and multiple layers of academic accreditation; which, at bottom-line, requires an acceptance of the reductionistic mental health conceptualization of the human person.

The State goes so far as to forbid a person not under its licensed control to use erstwhile *soul terms* when working with the public. Thus the terms *psychology* and *psychiatry* have been co-opted by the mental health system. While psychology traditionally means "study of the soul" and psychiatry means "treatment of the soul" (GK., ψυχή, psyche, soul), the mental health professions and mental health system formally excise the soul. Thus it is the State, being in total control of these professions and system, that is ultimately in total control of the clinical use of these soul-based terms. The State, in illicitly claiming ownership over these soul-based terms, has rendered their original meanings obsolete. In doing so, the State has sought to render the soul itself obsolete; thus reducing the person down to a completely quantifiable, that is manipulable, that is controllable, that is enslavable, entity. The State, in effect, has stolen the soul!

The mental health system has a rigid, non-negotiable default conceptualization of the human person that is reductionistic as per a biological model. This reductionistic view of the human person is gravely deficient and dangerous because it does not recognize the essential spiritual, psychomoral essence of the person which is of the soul. As such, the given mental health system's philosophical or qualitative conceptualizations remain necessarily inaccurate, superficial, grossly deficient, and ultimately iatrogenic, and any good they may do is haphazard, and only in spite of its reductionistic conceptualizations.

The State enforces this reductionistic view by statutory coercion and by monetary control via the insurance and pharmaceutical industries. Bottom-line: when it comes down to statutory discipline, professional ethics, or financial recompense, licensed mental health practitioners simply *must* abide by the "bible" of the mental health system, which is the reductionistic *Diagnostic & Statistical Manual* (*DSM*), and all other theories or elements are held to be either irrelevant, invalid, or unacceptable.

Note that the *mental health field* and its professions—be it psychology, psychiatry, or counseling—are taken here as a definitive whole. Though in specifics they may differ, these specifics are considered inessential. Practitioners may be allowed their quirks of conceptualization, so long as they ultimately ascribe to the mental health system's bottom-line and overriding reductionistic conceptualization of "mental health." If a discipline or practice is not subsumable and subordinate to that reductionistic view, it is not acceptable as part of the mental health system.

Brutalizing & Enslaving Reductionism

The mental health system's reduction, and thus violence unto, the human person is done in many ways: be it the reducing of essential human mal-being to mere symptomatic mental disordering; the reducing of a person to a helpless victim of a "mental disease" or of his past trauma; the reducing of the person to mere quantifiable physicality; the reducing of the person as a value that is either a functional or dysfunctional unit of society; and indeed, even the reducing of doctors and supposed healers of the soul to agents of the State or corporation.

Psychological reductionism involves the valuing, or more aptly devaluing, of the person as the sum total of his measurable parts. The reductionistic climate of the mental health system compels practitioners to treat their patients as the sum of their physical parts even if these practitioners do not in theory view their patients that way; for again, the pervasive view of the mental health intelligentsia (psychologists and psychiatrists) and the *de facto* practice of the mental health system (State, insurance, and pharmaceutical complex) do view the person as such and nothing more. There is the abiding belief in the mental health field that someday there will be no mystery at all to the person, but that each person will be easily understood in accord with his biological, physiological, and chemical components. It is this very reduction of the human down to mere organicity, to mere physical components, to the quantifiable, that has not only prevented the mental health system from being effective in treating its designated objective of mental symptomology, but has caused it to be a primary purveyor of grave harm both psychomorally, socially, and politically.

The following reasoning is representative of the mental health system's reduction of the human person down to pure physiology:

> The doctrine of the ghost in the machine is that people are inhabited by an immaterial soul that is the locus of free will and choice and which can't be reduced to a function of the brain. . . . But neuroscience is showing that all aspects of mental life—every emotion, every thought pattern, every memory—can be tied to the physiological activity or structure of the brain.[24]

---

24 S. Pinker, Cited in Callahan 2002.

This assertion that there is a neurological basis of all thought, feeling, and passion—that is, the physiology of the brain as the source and essence of personhood—is based on the logical fallacy of *equating correlation with causation*.

> It is quite possible that, from any mental activity, neuroscientists can abstract a mechanical aspect and associate it with certain thoughts, emotions, and so on. But that in no way "reduces" the mental activity to a "function of the brain." All that it demonstrates is that thinking, too, has a mechanical aspect to it. To move from that fact to the notion that those mechanical processes "cause" our thoughts is akin to deciding that, because we can abstract out certain aspects of any city and call that abstraction a "street map," that therefore street maps are the cause of cities![25]

While the attempt by psychologists and psychiatrists to reduce mental phenomenon—and hence the human person—down to physical units has something to do with their espousal of a philosophical ideology that is materialistic and even atheistic, the motive may be less philosophical and more utilitarian. In any case, the mental health system eliminates the essentially human, and thus the psychomoral etiological realm of essential well-being and mal-being, by coercively implementing a DSM medical model that, even if not truly medical, is still truly exclusive of the psychomoral. To so fit the person into this reductionistic medical

---

25 Callahan, G. 2002. *What Is Science?*
www.lewrockwell.com /callahan/callahan92.html

model, it is necessary to see the person as does a physician or, more aptly, a mechanic of the body: as a collection of tangible parts and components. However, as will be elaborated upon,[26] pretend as psychologists and psychiatrists might, the mental health DSM medical model is not medical; that is, it is not scientific.

Sad Practitioners

The maxim "physician heal thyself" is a valid criteria that avoids *ad hominem* fallacious connotations when the area to be healed is that physician's very specialty. In addition, psychomoralitics holds that an individual's reason and volition properly directed are capable of reducing mal-being, alleviating ego-reactivity, and, as a consequence, eliminating the superficial symptomology known as "mental disorder." Thus if a mental health clinician is unable to avoid or extricate himself from the throes of mental disorder, one might reasonably suspect that he would be unable to do so in others.

As an internal policy, the doctoral powerhouses of the mental health system in the United States—the American Psychological Association and the American Psychiatric Association—do not publicize statistical data for the "mental disorder" frequency of psychologists, nor the psychotropic drug use frequency of psychiatrists. If these statistics were published it is a sure bet that the public would be astounded and dismayed.

---

26 Chapter 3: § *The DSM Medical Model.* p.57

For psychologists are not able to heal themselves of the so-called mental disorders they treat through their psychotherapies, nor are psychiatrists able to function without themselves being chronically and increasingly self-medicated by the psychotropics they prescribe.

However, some worrisome statistics have leaked out concerning clinicians' own so-called "mental health." In regards to depression, a widely noted study from 1980 found that *73 percent of psychiatrists* had experienced moderate to incapacitating anxiety early in their careers, and *58 percent had suffered* from moderate to incapacitating depression. A study of more than 8,000 Finnish hospital employees found the psychiatric staff was *81 percent more likely* to suffer from a current or past mental illness and *61 percent more likely* to miss work due to depression. Compared to other female physicians, female psychiatrists have a *67 percent greater* likelihood of suffering from psychological problems, primarily depression. The study and/or statistics on the prevalence of depression, as well as other mental disorders, among psychologists has been suppressed. The suppression of such data is easily done by the profession of psychology since it is that profession's specific competency to compile such data and publish such studies.

In regards to suicide (*the* depressive act) psychologist David Lester, Ph.D., director of the Center for the Study of Suicide, states that *mental health professionals kill themselves at an abnormally high rate.* Indeed, highly publicized reports about the suicide rate of psychiatrists led the American Psychiatric Association to create a Task Force on Suicide Prevention in the late 1970s. A study initiated by that task force, published in 1980, concluded that *"psychiatrists commit suicide at rates about twice those expected [of physicians]"* and that *"the occurrence of suicides by psychiatrists is quite constant year-to-year, indicating a relatively stable over-supply of depressed psychiatrists."* No other medical specialty yielded such a high suicide rate. The only published data—now nearly 25 years old—on actual suicides among psychologists showed a rate of suicide for female psychologists that's *three times* that of the general population, although the rate among male psychologists was not higher than expected by chance. But suicide has been a tradition in the second and third tracks of clinical psychology and psychiatry, including such luminaries as Freud, Bettelheim, Federn, Stekel, Tausk, and Kohlberg.

Commonly a person's essential interpersonal relationship is with his spouse. Thus the marital relationship is a prime indicator of the relational aspect of essential-well being and symptomatic mental health. The divorce rate for psychiatrists from as early as the 1950s was *51 percent higher* than that of the general population and substantially higher than the rate in any other branch of medicine.[27] The study and/or statistics on the divorce rate of psychologists has, again, been suppressed.

---

27 From a study of the divorce rate for psychiatrists who graduated from Johns Hopkins University School of Medicine between 1948 and 1964. Klag, M., M.D.; 1977.

In a survey by Guy and James Liaboe, Ph.D., for example, psychotherapists themselves said they were hesitant to enter therapy,

> Because of feelings of embarrassment or humiliation, doubts concerning the efficacy of therapy, previous negative experiences with personal therapy, and feelings of superiority that hinder their ability to identify their own need for treatment.

Others believe, as many patients do, that seeking psychotherapy is a sign of failure. Here again, psychomoralitics proffers an answer. For psychomoralitics views the psychomoral state on a continuum and requires that its practitioners not only show that they are able to successfully undergo a course of it, but—and this is what "successful" truly means—continue the process in a habitual, and ever deeper manner for the rest of their lives.

As will be seen, in psychomoralitics the relevancy of a clinician's psychomoral, indeed personal and spiritual state, is crucial for clinical efficacy both in diagnosis and treating therapants. A psychomoralist must be able to enter into the subjective experience of the therapant and indeed model for them the ability to suffer-well the barbs of reality. Even more so, a psychomoralist is asked to avoid compartmentalization, but rather peacefully incorporate the therapant's suffering into his own life's spectrum of suffering. Conversely, mental health professionals that are trained to compartmentalize not only their client's sufferings, but their own suffering, risk the eventual debilitating failure of this compartmentalizing coping and limit their openness to reality, which has consequences both personally, clinically, and socially.

The Weaponization of the Mental Health Professions

The mental health professions are completely controlled by the State, and the insurance and pharmaceutical industries, rendering these professions systemically corrupt. This State/industrial control means that licensed practitioners, and thus their patients as well, are under the complete control of this State-insurance-pharmaceutical cabal. This licensing means that a licensed practitioner is first and foremost an agent of the State, even to the detriment of his patients. Required licensing is intrinsically unethical when applied to "talk therapy" or dialogic interventions such as mentoring, spiritual direction, psychotherapy, or any humanistic counseling discipline. In these disciplines there is no question here of public health, of tainted medicine, or faulty products, for all that is conveyed is an interpersonal relationship and words. State censoring of thoughts and words as "unhealthy" is not only a totalitarian nightmare of dystopian proportions, but absolutely unnecessary in that any ancillary malfeasance of a practitioner engaged in the above dialogic endeavors is covered by civil and criminal law.

The intrinsically unethical nature of licensing by the State of the humanistic counseling disciplines is egregiously demonstrated in the complete destruction of the most sacrosanct ethical principles of the therapeutic relationship: that of confidentiality.

All State licensed mental health providers must archive all records and notes and these must be turned over for *any reason and at any time* when so ordered by either the State, the courts, licensing boards, or in any hostile litigation against a patient (this hostile litigant is most often the State itself or a spouse in a divorce or custody case), even if contrary to a patient's wishes or harmful to his good. Thus there is *absolutely zero patient confidentiality* or privacy upheld in the mental health profession.

All practitioners, but especially humanistic counseling practitioners who are privileged to be entrusted with the most dramatic and intimate aspects of a person's existence, have ethical and moral obligations that entail the deepest reverence for, and ensuing protection of, the precious mystery that is the human person. This reverence not only "seeks to do no harm," but entails a *noblesse oblige* where the clinician will willingly suffer the slings and arrows of all, including the State, who would exploit his privileged relationship with those under his care.

The corrupt mental health system has, in addition to this unconscionable destruction of confidentiality and the sacrosanct clinical relationship, abused human rights as well. Most notably, investigative journalism uncovered the American Psychological Association's clandestine purveyance of psychological and physical torture in the service of the United States' covert and unconstitutional governmental operations.

> The APA's complicity in the CIA torture program,
> by allowing psychologists to administer and calibrate
> permitted harm, undermines the fundamental

ethical standards of the profession. If not carefully understood and rejected by the profession, this may portend a fundamental shift in the profession's relationship with the people it serves.[28]

Such outrageously unethical and inhumane practices can be seen as but the tip of the iceberg of a systemically corrupt system. However, that corruption is fully sanctioned and protected by the State and at least tacitly approved by the mental health professions, thus rendering that which is intrinsically immoral, professionally ethical.

As already mentioned, eerily and alarmingly, the State claims full statutory rights over the very use of the term *psychology*, as well as its practice. Thus the State and its mental health system now owns the term "psychology"; that is, the State and its mental health system owns the very study and treatment of the soul! This co-opting of the study and treatment of the soul by the State and its mental health system has allowed the State to, in effect, steal the soul from its citizens; for the State recognizes not the

---

28 *Report to the Special Committee of the Board of Directors of the American Psychological Association, An Independent Review Relating to APA Ethics Guidelines in National Security Interrogations and Torture*; Hoffman, D,. et al., July 7, 2015. This independent review revealed extensive details on how members of the American Psychological Association were complicit in torture and lied and covered up their close collaboration with officials at the Pentagon and CIA and modified the association's ethical guidelines so as to allow psychologists to participate in the government's so-called "enhanced interrogation programs." The report undermines the APA's repeated denials that some of its members were complicit in torture.

soul. Thus the State, through its weaponized mental health system, has accomplished statutorily the very separation of nature and grace, of body and soul, indeed of the image of God from man. Statutorily, no longer is the human person seen as a hylomorphic (soul-body) being whose essence transcends the worldly powers that be.

Chemical Straitjackets

The mental health system standardly and haphazardly uses psychotropics for the masking of symptomatic mental disorder. Psychotropics are used by the mental health system for everything from substitutes for child discipline, to chemical straitjackets, to punishments imposed by Orwellian "mental health courts." While it is irrefutable that psychotropics are dangerous both physically, psychomorally and spiritually, and have a caustic effect therein on those that take them, warnings or repudiations of psychotropic therapy by licensed professionals are nonetheless highly discouraged and even considered "unethical."

While the State will vigorously prosecute the mere words of one of its licensed psychotherapists it considers politically incorrect and thus harmful to a patient, it nonetheless turns a blind eye to the often lethal harm, both to the patient and others, caused by psychotropics. But while a medicated population is an easily controlled population, it is neither a psychomorally well nor a spiritually free population.

After the public outcry due to the epidemic of drug induced suicides, the FDA was finally forced to require the drug industry to place a "black box" label on all antidepressants warning of the increased risk of suicide. The medical profession itself has stated,

> Nearly all patients who remain on these chemical agents [psychotropics] for many years will develop some symptoms of CBI [Chronic Brain Injury]. . . . Each of these reactions can worsen the individual's mental condition and can result in suicidality, violence, and other forms of extreme abnormal behavior.[29]

Indeed, according to non-publicized findings from the American Psychiatric Association itself, those diagnosed with schizophrenia—the granddaddy of mental health diagnoses—and have the wherewithal to go contrary to the APA and remain unmedicated by psychotropics "have a significant better global functioning than those on anti-psychotics,"and have a much, much higher recovery rate, 40% vs. 5%, as well.[30] Yet this very same American Psychiatric Association advances with absolute certitude that such a diagnosis requires medication for the rest of one's life.

---

29 *International Journal of Risk & Safety in Medicine*, 23: 193-200; Breggin P R, 2011, Psychiatric drug induced Chronic Brain Impairment (CBI).

30 *American Psychiatric Association;* Presentation, Harrow, M.; 2008.

Primary Purveyor of Perversity

Finally, the mental health system has become the State's magisterium, its infallible arbitrator of morality. When what is good and true for the human person can be determined by a controlled and corrupt academic elite, and statutorily enforced as per adherence to nebulous professional ethical standards, then the worst sort of legal and moral positivism occurs. Indeed, the American Psychological Association and the American Psychiatric Association are leading purveyors of perversity, social reconstruction, and a brave new morality contrary not only to the historic morality of Western Civilization, but to the morality and mores of all civilized peoples.

The mental health system has waged an unceasing war against the intrinsic nature of the human person and natural law. Specifically, it has attacked traditional morality, the traditional and natural family, God-given gender, and thus human nature itself. Disingenuously, the mental health system has waged this demonic war under the banner of "human freedom and dignity." But *human freedom* and *dignity* are but the mental health system's doublespeak for *human degradation*. The human person with his ability to assent to truth, choose the good, and transcend his lower nature, is degraded by the mental health system to the mere status of a victim, be it a victim of his circumstances and/or biology. The mental health system further degrades the human person to a soul-less being, having as his essence the ego, that is his irrational pride and self-love; that is, Freud's infamous *id*. Yes, the mental health system aims to degrade the human person to a mere barnyard animal, an animal who is encouraged to be free to choose whatever decadent sty it wishes to wallow in. This is all good for the State and the powers that be, for those that are but victims are helpless, those that are but egos are manipulable, and those that are but animals are enslavable and can ultimately be led to slaughter.

Providentially, psychomoralitics provides the serendipitous antidote to the plethora of ills and evils caused by the mental health system. In freeing its therapants from innermost psychomoral bondage, psychomoralitics concurrently facilitates their freedom from the bondage of ego enhancing and manipulating psychotherapies, and from psychotropic constraints and anesthetizations. In doing so, psychomoralitics as well enables the insight and courage requisite for the freeing of oneself from political and social bondage, including the toxic bondage of the mental health system.

3. DIVERGENT DISCIPLINES

PSYCHOMORALITICS IS AN INNOVATIVE SOUL-DEEP SCIENCE that differs diametrically in paradigm from that of the mental health disciplines. But the psychomoralitic paradigm is innovative only in that it is foundationally *not* innovative. Unlike the mental health disciplines, psychomoralitics springs from the authentic scientific lineage of experimental and philosophical psychology.

Psychomoralitics' conceptual dynamics are ensconced between philosophical psychology and the experimental psychology that sprang from philosophical psychology. Though historically the scientific development of psychomoralitics has come much later, psychomoralitics is conceptually located between the lineage of a pure philosophical psychology and that of an empirical experimental psychology. But not so the mental health methodologies, which were severed at inception from the philosophical-experimental lineage and took deviant paths away from that lineage.

Philosophical psychology, especially in its anthropology and epistemology, studies qualitative truth about the human person. Most pertinent for an applied psychology *qua* soul-science (*viz.*, psychomoralitics), this qualitative truth expostulates upon *how* a person knows, wills, and thinks. On the other hand, experimental psychology studies quantitative mental and behavioral phenomena; that is, *manifestations* of how a person knows, wills, and thinks. Psychomoralitics, in treating essential mal-being and ego-reactivity, has both scientific philosophical qualitative origins and experimental quantitative manifestations.

Experimental psychology in its vigorous inception remained integrally connected with the science of philosophical psychology from which it sprang. However, over time experimental psychology became less united academically with philosophical psychology. Though this lack of overlap between philosophical and experimental psychologies was detrimental to both, its truly grave ramifications were in a nascent clinical psychology being alienated at its inception from that philosophical psychology. Though "running rats" without a proper philosophical understanding of sensate beings may have relatively benign ramifications, treating the soul without a proper, or even devoid, philosophical understanding of the psychomoral realm has grave ramifications indeed.[31]

The Original Applied Psychological Matrix

Unlike the later founders of the mental health disciplines, the founders of experimental psychology were firmly grounded in the philosophical psychology and anthropology of Western

---

31 Though the discipline of clinical psychology severely deviated from its origins, it still maintains an ironic remnant of its erstwhile grounding in experimental psychology and ultimately philosophical psychology with its *Doctor of Philosophy* (Ph.D.) degree.

civilization. Thus in the development of their experimental psychology, these founders were afforded a time tested and highly validated base of deductive knowledge that guided their application of the inductive empirical method. As true scientists, and thus cognizant of their areas of competency and incompetency, these founders would never have dared make up their own philosophy. Indeed, these scientists held that philosophy itself was a proper science, even *the science*[32] and, like all science, could be good or bad science. As such, experimental psychology was—as psychomoralitics itself is—built upon the perennial philosophical science of the West.

The father of experimental physiology and physiological psychology—and hence the grandfather of experimental psychology and the great-grandfather of psychomoralitics—is Johannes Müller (1801–1858). In Müller's opus magnus *Handbuch der Physiologie des Menschen für Verkesungen* (1834), experimental physiology is developed out of—and thus is inseparable from—Thomistic philosophical psychology and anthropology.

This adherence to Thomism resulted in Müller being a staunch proponent of the non-physiological component of man or the hylomorphic (soul/body) anthropological composition. Müller held that this hylomorphic anthropology was absolutely crucial to a proper understanding of any human phenomenon. Like all of the great foundational scientists of the empirical psychologies, Müller did not find it necessary to prove his empirical credentials

---

32 Science: a systematized and integral field of knowledge.

by denigrating the non-empirical. Indeed, upon his death
Müller's national obituary read:

> Unspoiled by the glory and renown which were
> his he never wavered for a moment from his firm
> and humble faith of his boyhood; in public and
> private he was the most religious of men, and the
> deeper he pierced into the secrets of science, the
> more ardently he cried out in praise of the wisdom
> and greatness of God.[33]

Building on Müller's legacy his disciple, Wilhelm Wundt
(1832–1920), founded experimental psychology. In 1879, Wundt
established the first formal laboratory for psychological research
at the University of Leipzig and was key in establishing
experimental psychology as a specific academic field, since it
uniquely drew on both philosophical psychology and the
empirical sciences. Like his mentor Müller, Wundt held that
empirical and experimental psychology was dependent upon
philosophical psychology.[34]

Wundt's co-founder of experimental psychology was Desiré
Mercier (1851–1926), a Belgian scholar and priest at the
University of Louvain who was later elevated to the cardinalate.
Cardinal Mercier's *Les Origines de la Psychologie Contemporaine*
(1897) was a history of true psychology as well as an application
of Thomism to the then current state of experimental psychology.

---

33 As quoted in Misiak, H., and V. M. Staudt. 1954. *Catholics in Psychology: A
  Historical Survey*. New York: McGraw-Hill, 1954.

34 See Chapter 4: § *Subalternation,* p.80

Like all of his co-founders, Mercier would firmly hold that experimental psychology was an auxiliary, or subalternated science to philosophical psychology and anthropology. Like Müller, Mercier would continually warn of the dangers inherent in adopting materialistic monism in experimental psychology; that is, he warned against a psychology that was reductionistic— not hylomorphic—and cut adrift from the perennial philosophy.

But cut adrift experimental psychology eventually was. An anti-scholastic, anti-philosophical, and maybe more so anti-Catholic reaction would cause the matrix of modern psychology to be denatured and poisoned. This matrix, divorced from applied psychology's original matrix, would be fueled by an ideological reaction that would seek to jettison all previous Western philosophical wisdom in the name of empirical science. From this rootless and deviant matrix sprang today's mental health disciplines which, instead of growing to maturation in integral relation within an inherent and interstitial philosophical and experimental scientific matrix, would have an arbitrary and aberrant development. Being totally alienated from philosophical psychology, due in part to experimental psychology's increased distance from that philosophical psychology, the mental health disciplines were destined to become an unsystematized mishmash of superficial conceptualizations; that nonetheless are united in their common foundational deficiency and grave deviant error.

Thomas Aquinas (1225-1274)

Johannes Müller (1801–1858)

Wilhelm Wundt (1832–1920)

Desiré Mercier (1851–1926)

The Deviant Mental Health Disciplines

Though deficient in a foundation in philosophical psychology, what remains that is scientific about the mental health disciplines is empirical clinical observation, superficial though these observations may be. For instance, Freud's case studies were impressive in their observation of repressed psychomoral conflict manifested psychosomatically; Skinner's detailed measurements were impressive in predicting conditioned behavior; and the medical or biological model recognizes and categorizes overt empirical symptomology. Indeed, most all of the popular personality theories, psychotherapies, and psychiatries get right the recognition and labeling of superficial symptomology and the constellations of symptomology, of personality types and temperaments, of behavioral patterns and behavioral quirks. But the empirical part is the obvious, and thus easy part. What's more, all of these valid empirical elements go wildly awry in the mistaken placement of them as etiology; a mistake of hubris that arrogantly measures all things by the limits of a particular knowledge or discipline.

In clinical psychology, noticing symptoms, disorders, failures, eccentricities, moods, etc. is easy. What is difficult is the identification of the essential causes of these symptoms, which is the prerequisite for discovering their remedy. However, it is not only difficult, but fool-hardy to attempt to find the cause and thus cure of disordered mental symptomology without first having in place an adequate philosophical anthropology that can produce a correct topography of the underlying psychomoral realm. The early theorists such as Freud, Adler, Jung, *et al.* were creative, however, they began with a willful ignorance/arrogance, or even ideological rejection, of the very philosophical matrix that gave rise to the experimental psychology that, in turn, gave rise to their applied clinical psychology.

While the original founders of modern empirical and experimental psychology prudently and scientifically built upon the philosophical wisdom of the ages, the founders of today's applied mental health psychology imprudently overreached their competency in an attempt to develop a completely new and independent science, when in fact it was a new science mostly dependent on an old one. What resulted was the dominant applied mental health psychologies with their various deviant formulations. These formulations were a creative but haphazard endeavor. The dominant applied psychologies' formulations hammered together theories of so-called "mental disorder" and "personality theory" to fit the symptomology observed, or, worse yet, the personality of the theorists themselves.

In scornful reaction to these often elaborate and ever morphing creative conceptualizations were other applied psychology deviations that adopted an extremely deficient *reductionistic* anthropology. These reductionistic applied psychologies were originally dominated by behavioralism and then finally by the medical/biological basis model. But both the elaborate personality theories and the reductionistic theories were based on the empirical observation of superficial symptoms, be they mentations or behaviors. In both conceptualizations, gross empirical observation reigns supreme, and insightful philosophical reasoning gravely lacks. Thus the mental health field possesses an inherent tendency towards an unscientific subjectivity due to its superficial objectivity, resulting in a never ending revision and interpretation that is found in the plethora of personality theories, as well as in the ever morphing biological theory. As will be seen, without a philosophical and deductive objectivity, the empirical—scientific—inductive method is at loose ends indeed.

Deviant Personality Theories

In place of a comprehensive examination of clinical psychology's many innovative personality theories, that of Sigmund Freud's (1856–1939) will rightly be taken as representative, for it is the first, most impacting, and arguably most creative of all. Indeed, Freud was to establish the egoistic (i.e., *id*) enhancing orientation and foundation that is the *sine qua non* of the mental health professions today. Though many of today's mental health practitioners are not dogmatically Freudian they all, if merely as members of the mental health system, stand upon this faulty egoistic enhancing orientation and foundation.

Freud was a product of the West, and specifically a stepchild of highly refined Catholic Austria, and he drew on that culture's psychomoral understanding of the human person. Specifically, Freud naturally accepted that there was an underlying dynamic to human behavior. Yet Freud was trained as a neurologist and, notwithstanding his ambient cultural inculcation, was formally untrained in philosophy. More so, Freud became extremely hostile to his culture, both the weak ethnic Judaism of his family and the strong cultural Catholicism of his society, and thereby explicitly rejected their somewhat kindred morality and philosophy. Freud was also famously haunted by his own dysfunctional childhood and subsequent psychomoral mal-being.

Freud's true genius was as a creative writer, which was displayed in his brilliant efforts to produce a consistent narrative of his psychological and personality theories. Freud's theories, which were constantly under revision, were an attempt to explicate as empirical scientific principles his own particular mal-being and personality malformation, as well as those of his patients. In doing so, he creatively remixed the Western philosophical anthropology he had culturally imbibed. The result was Freud's topsy-turvy psychodynamic topography, a mishmash of the traditional Western understanding of the underlying psychomoral essence of the human person.

The traditional Western conceptualization (being similar to most other cultures) is that the psyche from which emanates the psychomoral agency of the reason and will is the essence of the human person, and that this agency is somehow hampered by an egoistic concupiscence and viciousness. Freud held the reverse. Freud made the ego with its concupiscence and viciousness the essence (viz., the *id*) of the person and psychomoral agency (viz., *super ego*) of the psyche an overweening and hampering encumbrance. In practice, this allowed Freud to make normative not only the psychomoral mal-being (especially psychosexual) of his patients, but of his own mal-being. As such, Freud's psychotherapy was about strengthening the pseudo-self of the ego[35] by enabling its coping mechanisms and passions to function well. This strengthening of the pseudo-self remains, be it recognized or not, the common psychotherapeutic goal of all the psychological and psychiatric conceptualizations of the mental health professions. As will be seen, such an egocentric, or rather ego-essential, conceptualization is diametrically opposed to psychomoralitics.

Freud's work, even though under constant revision, was doomed to fail in clinical efficacy, if not in popularity, since in essence it was a work of fiction. Freud's own prejudice and reaction against the corpus of perennial Western philosophy assured this failure. An example of this fictional development and prejudicial reaction can be found in Freud's adoption of Helmholtzian physics' *law of the conservation of energy.* This theory provided the template for Freud's "psychic energy model," which is the very foundational principle of Freudian psychology. Freud, like many of his contemporaries, unreservedly embraced any theory on the merit that it was perceived, even if mistakenly, to be materialistic, atheistic, or anti-scholastic.

Thus Freud creatively placed the lower science of physics, specifically the then cutting edge Helmholtzian theory, into the placeholder of the higher science of philosophical anthropology.

---

35 See Chapter 5: *Psychomoralitic Topography.* p.85

However, in doing so Freud betrayed the very academic integrity of the Helmholtzian model. For Herman Helmholtz (1821–1894) was a disciple of the aforementioned Johannes Müller and, like his master, strictly adhered to the hylomorphic anthropological composition of the human person. Helmholtz would have been aghast at the idea of applying his principles of physics and energy conservation to the psychomoral realm of the person.

Like Freud, the subsequent plethora of personality theorists were at best competent in observing and classifying symptomology and would thus make some useful discoveries as to clinical techniques and symptom description. But again, like Freud, they would also hold in common their rejection, or at least unawareness, of the perennial Western philosophical anthropology of the human person. Even William James (1842–1910), considered the father of the psychology of religion because of his openness to spirituality (and the inspiration of the failed Protestant attempts to integrate Christianity and clinical psychology), sardonically said in his seminal work *Varieties of Religious Experience*,[36]

> [I]f we could descend on our subject from above like Catholic theologians, with our fixed definitions of man and man's perfection and our positive dogmas about God, we should have an easy time of it.

Here James tellingly fails to distinguish between philosophy and theology, and even religious dogma. But in any case, James, and all the other founders and followers of the deviant disciplines

---

36 Lecture XIV.

of the mental health profession, chose to make up their definitions as they went along instead of accessing the concise scientific definitions of the psychomoral nature of man found in the West's philosophical patrimony.

Again James, like Freud and many others, does not make a distinction between philosophy and theology. Rather there is the mistaken belief that because one rejects religious dogma one must reject any concomitant philosophy as well. In this case, such a position led to the grievous jettisoning of the most venerable and perennial Western philosophical thought, a tragedy that eventually led to the mental health cabal itself. James here also holds the characteristic deviant applied psychologies' promotion of induction in the place of deduction.[37] Even someone like James, with his much touted "spiritual sense," is more inductive than deductive since that "spiritual sense" originates in a subjective experience rather than emanating and deduced from natural law and reality.[38]

Like Freud and James, the plethora of personality theorists' antagonism toward the old, or maybe just their desire for the new, fueled the non-circumspect rejection of the perennial

---

37 Deductive reasoning works from the more general to the more specific. Inductive reasoning works from specific observations to broader generalizations and theories.

38 But deduction itself is not only objective but very commonsensical because it is both logical and universally observable. Thus deductive logical conclusions will intersect with both commonsense and inductive observation, a combination that is especially advantageous for clinical intervention and is present in the discipline of psychomoralitics.

philosophy of the West. While the mental health field, and academia as well, are today at times open to "spiritualities or philosophies" (especially those of an Eastern bent), they still recoil most viscerally, if not intellectually, at the thought of even a systematic scientific philosophy that has anything remotely to do with traditional Christianity.[39] It is as if the mental health field, and the empirical sciences in general, are still recoiling from their breakup with their first and formative relationship[40] with Catholic academia, and now anything reminiscent of that former intimacy must be eradicated or rejected.[41]

But because the human person remains the same today as yesterday, the jettisoning of an understanding of the human person, indeed of reality, that was integrally developed and defined over the centuries is reckless at best. But more so, such a jettisoning has grave consequences clinically; for the efficacy of

---

39 A person need not be Western, much less a Christian, to avail himself of psychomoralitics. For a person to avail themselves of the psychomoralitic process they need only be human (again, rationality and volition are the specific human difference). A person's worldview or beliefs do not change his nature. Though subjective views and beliefs of a therapant are important clinical factors, it is upon the objective given nature of the human person that psychomoralitics effects transformation, and that in turn aligns subjective views and beliefs to objective reality as well.

40 The advent of the modern university system itself took place under the auspices of Catholic academics. See Woods, T.E.; *How the Catholic Church Built Western Civilization*; Regnery Publishing, 2005.

41 Though psychomoralitics directly derives from philosophy and not theology, it must be recognized that there is a very real danger of academia's prejudicial rejection of psychomoralitics because its anthropology was cultivated and perfected within European Christendom.

any applied psychology depends specifically on both a proper understanding of the psychomoral nature of the human person and the reality he is called to encounter.

Reductionistic Theories

The more reductionistic, and thus less essentialist, a psychological theory is, the more likely it does not espouse the overt philosophical error that so plagues the more elaborate personality theories. However, a reductionistic theory does cause catastrophic errors of deficiency and/or omission. Indeed, such a reductionism eviscerates the human person of his very essence! This essential evisceration of the person is found exactly in reductionism's dogmatic rejection of all that is beyond its realm of competency, a realm which is the quantifiable of material empiricism.

Note well: that which is within quantifiable psychology's competency is not in itself invalid, be it an experimental psychology's statistical norms, a behaviorism's observation of external effects, or a psychiatry's compilation of physiological symptomology. Rather quantifiable psychology's error, and especially clinical psychology's most grave error, is in reducing the conceptualization of the human person down to the parameters of its competency. Further error is also found in the supposed "empirical" theories, such as the *chemical imbalance theory*, which are manifestly not based on solid empirical evidence but rather are creatively extrapolated from mere symptomology.

Being reductionistic in regards to an applied humanistic psychological conceptualization is to doom treatment to failure. When the person is reduced down to his physiology, and even more so his mere brain chemistry, then the determinative psychomoral realm remains untreated. The prevalent theory in the mental health field in the twenty first century is the reductionistic medical model. The highly esteemed and societally preeminent profession of medicine, in union with the incredibly wealthy pharmaceutical and insurance industries and the all-powerful coercive State, has successfully proselytized the West into accepting this reductionistic medical model of mental health.

But before the medical profession espoused the reductionistic medical model, it just as devotedly espoused the highly elaborate personality theory of Freudianism and other variant schools of psychoanalysis. Freud and his spawns were accepted by the medical profession as saviors and their devised theories as gospel. There was indeed a certain religiosity involved in being admitted into psychoanalytic practice. In addition to studies, no less than five years of psychoanalysis partaken of three times a week was required in the rite of initiation. So too, the psychoanalytic discipline worked zealously to limit admission to its ranks to medical doctors, thus making it even more rarefied. Today a similar exclusivity can be seen as the psychiatric discipline works even harder to limit the dispensing of its psychotropic sacraments to duly ordained physicians.

The religion of Freudianism experienced a great apostasy among its psychiatric priesthood after its heyday in the 1960s (the '60s actually being the Freudian *id* unleashed culturally) with the advent of psychotropics. It was much easier, quicker, antiseptic, and profitable to write a script for psychotropics than to train in and administer psychoanalysis.[42] The medical profession had nothing less than a reactionary swing from the elaborate psychoanalytic model to the new reductionistic, medical, biological, pharmaceutical model. This reaction seems in part due to psychiatry's understandable professional embarrassment for its once zealous adoption of psychoanalysis as a valid scientific theory.

But the foolhardy gullibility of the medical profession in regards to its once wholehearted and indeed dogmatic acceptance of Freudianism is not surprising. With the diminishing of classical liberal arts and philosophical coursework in the mid-twentieth century collegiate curricula, coupled with the increased undergraduate specialization that was spearheaded by the pre-medical major, physicians tended to be especially deficient in the classical liberal arts and philosophical training. So too, having embraced the dogma of psychoanalysis, including its creative anthropologies (most especially the fiction of Freudianism), medical psychiatry was extremely wary of venturing again into the philosophical and psychomoral realm where it was so badly

---

42 Indeed, instead of undergoing five days per week of psychoanalysis, medical model psychiatrists merely had to avail themselves of daily free lunches and yearly, all expenses paid, educational junkets provided by the deep-pocketed pharmaceutical industry.

duped before. This wariness is indeed warranted, for psychiatry has no competency in those philosophical and psychomoral realms. The vast majority of today's physicians are philosophically illiterate, and subsequently not even aware that a perennial philosophical anthropology of the human person even exists. In any case, psychiatry's reaction to the error of psychoanalysis is the new and equally arrogant error of excluding and invalidating those higher sciences in which it has no competency, and holding as valid only that in which it does have a competency.

The DSM Medical Model

> Note: There are ample varied, detailed, and damning critiques by psychiatrists (see Appendix C), psychologists, and laypersons accessible in regards to the DSM medical model. As such, the following critique will be brief and highlight the DSM medical model's incongruity with the psychomoralitic conceptualization.

The mental health system's holy writ is the *Diagnostic and Statistical Manual* (*DSM.*) The DSM, reflecting the instability of the psychiatric discipline itself, has been constantly revised, going all the way from a strictly psychoanalytic paradigm to the so-called bio/medical model. Though the new and evolved DSM may be less an elaborate fiction than that of psychoanalytic literature, it nonetheless can still be regarded as a fiction. Though the DSM claims to be empirical, scientific and medical, these claims are only its desired goals, not its reality.

All mental disorders are contained within psychiatry's *Diagnostic and Statistical Manual of Mental Disorders*, and are arrived upon by psychiatrists literally voting on what is, or is not, considered a mental disorder. Unlike the rest of medicine, mental disorders are arrived at by a political, not a medical, process. In the United States, the nation's leading mental health organization is the National Institute of Mental Health (NIMH), and this is what the head of NIMH stated in 2013:

> While DSM has been described as a "Bible" for the field, it is, at best, a dictionary…. The weakness is its lack of validity. Unlike our definitions of ischemic heart disease, lymphoma, or AIDS, the DSM diagnoses are based on a consensus about clusters of clinical symptoms, not any objective laboratory measure. In the rest of medicine, this would be equivalent to creating diagnostic systems based on the nature of chest pain or the quality of fever.[43]

Thus the DSM "medical model" is not really medical. The medical model is a paradigm based on nosology (the classification of diseases) which is essential for diagnosis and treatment. The task in nosology is to define and classify diseases clearly. This is done most adequately when etiology (cause) and/or pathogenesis (the mechanism by which the disease is caused) are known. Diseases classified by symptomology[44] are not by themselves

---

43 Thomas Insel, Director, National Institute of Mental Health.

44 Alternatively, diseases may be classified according to the organ system involved, though this is often complicated since many diseases affect more than one organ.

valid medical nosologies. However, a nosology of descriptive symptomology is found in the DSM's categorization of mental disorders (as opposed to organic disorders[45]). The DSM nosology is somewhat of a fiction, and at best an educated guess, and deficient unto invalidity.

The criteria and classification system of the current DSM is based on a process of *consultation and committee meetings* involving psychiatrists and psychologists. The lead psychiatrist in the formulation of the DSM V openly admitted that there was little "scientific research" done to back up the diagnostic claims in the DSM.[46] When the first claimed medical model of the *Diagnostic and Statistical Manual* came out in 1980, it had purged itself of any remaining psychoanalytic content and added more mental illness categories with included criteria (i.e., descriptive symptomology). At that time, in its very introduction, the editors of the DSM issued a sort of disclaimer:

> For most of the DSM-III disorders, however, the etiology is unknown. A variety of theories have been advanced, buttressed by evidence—not always convincing—to explain how these

---

45 An important clarification is that the psychomoralitic conceptualization does not classify neurological and organic disorders as essential inner mal-being. The DSM, on the other hand, makes no such distinction between a psychological disorder and an organic impairment; classifying, for instance, both major depression and mental retardation as "mental disorders." When psychomoralitics uses essential mal-being it refers to that which has its etiology in the psychomoral realm, not that which has an organic etiology (such as brain injuries or learning disabilities).

46 First, M.B., see Chapter 2, *Epigraph*.

disorders came about. The approach taken in
DSM-III is atheoretical with regard to etiology or
pathophysiological process except for those
disorders for which this is well established and
therefore included in the definition of the disorder.
Undoubtedly, with time, some of the disorders of
unknown etiology will be found to have specific
biological etiologies, others to have specific
psychological causes, and still others to result
mainly from a particular interplay of
psychological, social, and biological factors.[47]

The Chemical Imbalance Fiction

In addition to the deficiency of the DSM nosology, matters
are made worse by the mental health field's wholesale adoption
of the "chemical imbalance" theory of mental disorder. In order
to make up for a deficient symptom based nosology the discipline
of psychiatry and the industry of pharmacology has claimed an
etiology of neurological chemical imbalance. The way they have
gone about this is even further from a medical model than a mere
symptom based nosology.

> Patients [sic] having been diagnosed with
> "chemical imbalances" despite the fact that no test
> exists to support such a claim, and that there is no
> real conception of what a correct chemical balance
> would look like. Patients with years of medication
> trials which have done nothing except reify in

47 DSM-III Introduction (p.7)

them an identity as a chronic patient with a bad brain. This identification as a biologically-impaired patient is one of the most destructive effects of biologic psychiatry.[48]

The main chemical imbalance theory of etiology is found in the mood disorder of major depression, with the *Selective Serotonin Uptake Inhibitors (SSRIs)* treatment being the prime example. Pharmacological companies developed a drug that, in theory, would impede serotonin from being reabsorbed into neurological tissue and thus increase its presence between the synapses of the neurons. Patients diagnosed with major depression were given this drug and there was often an alleviation of some symptomology. Therefore, the cause of depression was surmised to be a lack of serotonin between the neuro-synapses. There are no tests that can confirm this theory, and yet it is held out as fact by psychiatry and pharmacology. In addition, one of the side effects of the SSRIs is the very symptomology of depression it is supposed to alleviate!

Unlike a medical conceptualization's exclusion of psychomoral etiology, a psychomoral based conceptualization does not discount medical or physiological factors in ego-reactivity. However, even from a physiological perspective it is considered more efficacious to treat a person systemically (the entire physiology and hopefully etiology in the case of physical disorders) as opposed to treating mere symptoms. For example, it

---

48 Kaiser, D., M.D.; *Against Biologic Psychiatry; Psychiatric Times;* Dec. 1996, Vol. XIII, Issue 12.

is better to deal, if possible, with the systemic cause of a skin eruption than merely treating it with a steroidal symptom alleviator. So too, treatment aimed at symptom alleviation, like steroidal use, often causes both systemic harm and eventual exacerbation of symptomology.

The occurrence of systemic harm and exacerbation of symptomology with the use of psychotropics is definitive. Pharmacological companies have studies that show, for instance, that continued use of psychotropics makes a person more susceptible to the symptoms it seeks to alleviate.

> This even though there is publication bias, especially the lack of publication of negative treatment studies, is known to be a major problem in the medical literature. In particular, it appears that the pharmaceutical industry is not routinely making data from negative studies available through the published scientific literature.[49]

In short, the continued use of psychotropics almost insures that a "mental health diagnosis" becomes an incurable life-long sentence. As such, both reality blunting psychotropic therapy and self-esteem and ego building psychotherapy have this in common: *both fail to cure their "clients," but rather create an enslaving dependency in those clients.*

---

49 Ghaemi, S.N., M.D., MPH;   Shirzadi, A., DO; Filkowski, M., BA; 09/10/2008; Medscape.

4. Reality-Based Conceptualization

Psychomoralitics' very object of concern, both its promoting of essential well-being and human flourishing, as well as its rectifying of essential mal-being and ego-reactivity, differs from that of the mental health professions; professions that only address superficial mental or behavioral symptomology. But so too, psychomoralitics' very concept of "sanity," of being in touch with reality, differs from that of the mental health field. The psychomoralitic definition of essential well-being is keyed on reality: be that reality in the existential form of the *real*, or in the cognitive form of the *truth*, or in the volitional form of the *good*. Essential human well-being is found in a person's *receiving-the-real, assenting-to-truth, and choosing-the-good*. Thus the goal of psychomoralitics is itself strictly oriented to the real, the truth, and the good.

As will be seen, the *real/truth/good* is not only psychomoralitics' goal, but its cohesive principle and foundation as well. But this is not the case with the deviant disciplines of the mental health field. In general the mental health field has two defining measurements of mental health. Both are superficial at best, and both are gravely deficient. This superficiality and deficiency is due to the glaring omission in regards to the essential concept of reality. Essential well-being cannot be accurately recognized nor efficaciously treated without an essential understanding of reality; for reality (and this should be most obvious) is the very touchstone of any purported psychomoral well-being, and should be of any so-called "mental health" as well.

Mental Health Conceptualization

According to the *Diagnostic and Statistical Manual V*:

> A mental disorder is a syndrome characterized by clinically significant disturbance in an individual's cognition, emotion regulation, or behavior that reflects a dysfunction in the psychological, biological, or developmental processes underlying mental functioning. Mental disorders are usually associated with significant distress in social, occupational, or other important activities. An expectable or culturally approved response to a common stressor or loss, such as the death of a loved one, is not a mental disorder. Socially deviant behavior (e.g., political, religious, or sexual) and conflicts that are primarily between the individual and society are not mental disorders unless the deviance or conflict results from a dysfunction in the individual, as described above.[50]

Thus the mental health field's first measurement of its symptomatic mental disorder is along the line of functionality. This line of functionality is essentially a continuum of success and failure. If a person is successful in life he is considered functional;

---

50 APA, DSM-5 *Definition of a Mental Disorder* p.20

if a person is unsuccessful or a failure he is considered dysfunctional. But what is success? Though it may vary in nuances, success for the mental health system at bottom line means being communally, economically, and politically functional. Communal functionality entails family, friends, and others. Economic functionality is based on being somewhat of a producer,[51] and hence profitable consumer. Political functionality in the modern state basically means obeying positivistic (hence at times arbitrary or even immoral) laws[52] and staying out of legal trouble. While functionality can be an indicator that a person is encountering reality on a certain level, it is usually only a superficial level of measurement. Joseph Pieper (1989) wrote:

---

51 However the mental health system also recognizes, and indeed *functionally* thrives on, the very important *recipient victim*. The recipient victim depends on the State for his welfare, be it financial, personal, or sociopolitical. The recipient victim is dependently subservient to the State, thus empowering it and its bureaucracy. The recipient victim provides the State et al., with the ruse of benign caretaking. The recipient victim also provides the State et al., with another very useful and coercive placeholder, that of "perpetrator," who is the proclaimed nemesis of the State's recipient victim.

52 Legal positivism is a philosophy of law that imbues law with validity in accord with current conventions, which in practice means what is judicially or legislatively constructed and political imposed by the State. According to legal positivism, law is synonymous with whatever happens to be the positive or current judicial or legislative norms. Legal positivism holds law to be ultimately arbitrary and does not base it on any objective, immutable moral principles. Neither natural law, reason, nor inherent human rights are recognized by legal positivism. Legal positivism arose in opposition to Western Civilization's perennial natural law theory, which holds that there are objective, immutable moral principles that constrain and override positivistic and legislative law.

It insults the dignity of man's spirit to lead a life so much confined and imprisoned within narrow considerations of immediate usefulness that his own small environment utterly ceases to be a window on the larger "world." To be thus totally absorbed in a mere fragment of reality, to "function" rather than live, is not human....For life to be truly human it seems indispensable that every so often the domain of practical work and effectiveness be shaken up and brought down to size by the challenge, disturbing yet fruitful, coming from the world's ultimate reality.[53]

So mental health as functionality, success or failure, depends on how well adapted a person is to the mainstream: to the communal, financial, and political power structures that be. Such a functionality, though not necessarily (though it can be) bad, should not be the definitive hallmark in evaluating a person's mental and moral fitness, his sanity. Rather, the touchstone of such an evaluation should be a person's essential well-being, and this essential well-being should transcend political, financial, and relational variables. There is a great inherent danger to the human person when he is essentially evaluated as per the primary mental health value of adapting to the current political, economic, or social powers, especially when those powers or those in their employ are the evaluators (*read* judge, jury, and executioners) as well.

---

53 Pieper, Josef. *Living the Truth* (reprint). San Francisco: Ignatius Press, 1989.

The greatest danger of evaluating a person as per the mental health standard of functionality is the potential (and now fully actualized) weaponization of the mental health field as a coercive instrument of the State.[54] Indeed, psychomoralitics understands those who suffer most acutely from ego-reactivity (and the sometimes concurrent symptomology of mental disordering) as not only often marching to the beat of a different drummer, but as often having the potential to prophetically step-out against the powers-that-be.

The second continuum of mental health is that of a nebulous *feeling good*. Thus the standard lead-in question of any mental health session is: "So how have you been feeling?" with a *feeling good* being the sought after indicator of mental health. Aside from being solely based in subjectivism, a mere *feeling good* does not indicate true essential well-being. Rather essential well-being is indicated by the ability to *feel good or bad* as per an authentic, receptive, and peaceful encounter with reality. When a mere

---

54 The above DSM tautological disclaimer that *social deviation is not a mental disorder unless considered to be dysfunctional* is not soothing. Nor is it soothing, but quite chilling, to know that the *American Psychological Association* secretly collaborated with rogue agencies of the United States Federal government to implement, and legally and ethically justify, the torturing of prisoners. (Soldz, S., et. al.; *All the President's Psychologists: The American Psychological Association's Secret Complicity with the White House and US Intelligence Community in Support of the CIA's Enhanced' Interrogation Program.* April 2015.)

feeling good is the goal then people become superficial, for it is easiest to feel good on a superficial level.[55]

So too, the interplay of functionality, feeling good, and essential human well-being are confounding. Many of the rich and famous notoriously suffer from a bored self-pity characterized by *ennui* with depressive symptomology. So too, many of those who have achieved great success, that are optimally "functional," often are driven by nothing less than a pathological drive. Conversely, a person can be quite the worldly failure, but have a peaceful resignation and joy that rests in an assent to truth and love of the good that transcends values such as worldly success, popularity, or sociopolitical power. As for feeling good, a person may not feel good at all, may feel very bad about life or even himself, and yet feels this way because he is in touch with reality to a superlative degree. So too, a person can feel as good as a pig in mud while actually being mired in the mud and being more like a pig than a man. Thus essential human well-being cannot be accurately evaluated in accord with functionality and a nebulous good feeling.

Reality

The mental health profession is not only ignorant of the psychomoral realm and essential well-being, it is not even fully

---

55 By means of the selective reality of coping and the various drugs of choice available today (e.g., consumerism, entertainment, or psychotropics). See Chapter 8: *Egoistic Coping.* p.139

cognizant of reality! This is due to the absence of an ontological basis in the mental health conceptualization. *Ontology* is the study of *what is real*. As a result, the *Diagnostic and Statistic Manual* and the mental health field does not, and cannot, validly speak of reality. Commonsensically this deficiency is shocking: for again, *isn't reality the very touchstone of sanity?* Doesn't essential well-being, and freedom from mal-being and sometimes manifestation in disordered mental symptomology, have everything to do with how a person interacts with reality?

So too, because of this failure in ontology, even the goal of the mental health field is nebulous. The mental health field states its all-encompassing goal as the promoting of "health and human welfare" in "all aspects of the human experience." Though grandiose, this goal cannot be but an empty statement. For the mental health field is rendered unable to discern the real; and is thus unable to discern the truth and the good; and is thus unable to validly determine what is true and good for man; and is thus unable to discern what constitutes "health and human welfare."

So too, if there is no discernible ontology there can be no discernible *teleology* or *end* of the "human experience." For the very specific difference of the human person—that which essentially comprises the "human experience"—is the call to seek the real, the truth, and the good. Human teleology provides the very definition of essential human well-being; *viz.,* receiving-the-real, assenting-to-truth, and choosing-the-good.

Ontology, or the science of being, is not complicated. A person knows *being* intuitively, and continues to grow in that knowledge of *being, the real, truth,* and *good* if his mind is open and he is maturing psychomorally. But such an openness to reality is more common with the common man than with the academic elite, including mental health professionals, who often pride themselves on their skepticism. But this skepticism is not really skeptical at all; it is not really a disbelief but a very strong belief, indeed a blinding faith, that denies common sense reality.

Supreme Being

It suffices to say that the mental health system is such a dismal failure and deadly influence because it is Godless. The mental health system excludes conceptually even the basic philosophic premise of Supreme Being, and is thus *de facto* atheistic. But without a conceptualization based on Supreme Being, the mental health system cannot have a conceptualization based on analogous contingent being, and without a conceptualization of being, it cannot have a concept of the real, the true, and good.

To exclude, as does the mental health system both ideologically and as a bottom-line policy, the concept of a realm of Supreme Being[56] is to, at the very least, acquiesce to a close-minded dogmatism. For the atheistic position is premised on a blind faith that countermands logic and accepts the absurd. A person does

---

56 Supreme Being: A non-contingent being that is a first moving and ordering cause of the universe, and from which all other being analogously derives.

not believe but *knows*, in accord with the constructs of the human mind and its incessant demands of logic, that God exists. Whereas a person *believes*, but cannot know, that God does not exist. Atheistic belief, being illogical, is visceral. In atheistic belief, the egoistic passions well up and bind the intellect, with a hateful denial rather than a logical reasoning forming the conclusion. This is not to say that religious belief cannot itself be a reality denying "opiate," but that it need not be.

A close-minded atheism which rejects the possibility of a Supreme Being is untenable for the human intellect. Atheism specifically and necessarily does violence to human logic and leads to intellectual absurdity, as the modern existentialist's own conclusion of absurdity witnesses to. Even a mere agnostic non-entertainment of the question of a Supreme Being is restricting and stifling of the human intellect. For agnosticism is but a delaying tactic that ignores the most pressing issues of human existence and denies the human vocation of seeking the truth at its most absolute.

To believe there is no God, nothing uncreated and thus Supremely Real, is illogical because commonsensically, as well as philosophically, the order of the universe, and even the existence of the universe, must emanate from principles not found in the universe itself. The universe's coming into being, its being set in motion, commonsensically requires another realm or cause that is *totally other* than that of this universe and the realm of empirical existence. To hold that there is such a realm is not a belief but a logical necessity. Human reason knows, *if it can know anything at all*, that this realm of existence has not within it the principles of eternity; that it could not have just always been. Logically there must needs be another realm that is totally Other, that does have as its nature the quality of having always been. Thus the dictates of human logic require that there be a realm of being upon which the universe's very existence depends, otherwise human understanding necessarily falls into an inextricable web of absurdity.

While psychomoralitics as an applied humanistic science is not primarily concerned with defining the origins of the universe, it *is* concerned with opening a person up in a most radical manner to the real, including that which is beyond and apparently causative of empirical phenomenon. Psychomoralitics is also concerned with a person's assent to truth, an assent that is rendered null if logic is violated unto absurdity. Finally, psychomoralitics is concerned with a person's choosing of the good, a choosing which is totally arbitrary if there is no Supreme Good/Truth/Reality/Being. Thus it is a person's openness to, and subsequent embracing of reality that is forthwith demarcated.

A God Ordered Mind & Heart

Because for the human intellect an atheistic position entails a logical absurdity, and even an agnostic position entails the possibility of a logical absurdity, those that hold such positions necessarily do violence to the human reasoning process; and hence to the human concept of truth; and hence to the good and being itself; and hence to the human person as a truth seeker. Positing that God does not exist renders the human person as a *seeker of truth, good, and beatitude* empty and tragic indeed; leaving nothing deeper within a person than this emptiness, nor anything loftier outside a person than the sought after but illusory divine chimera. And therein lies the urgency of the ultimate quest to answer the ultimate dilemma, a quest into even an apparent emptiness.

It is thus *the process* of this ultimate questing that is the psychomoralitic entry into reality, bring what it may. The mere beginning of this quest already brings with it the psychomoralitic promise of innermost peace, for the prioritization of the quest brings due proportion to all particular aspects of a person's life in accord with the grand scheme of existence. Making an initial peace with the deepest yearnings of the human soul allows a person to carry on day-to-day in the more mundane particulars of existence; to in fact make these mundanities psychomoralitic.

For those that would deal with or treat the human person in his fullness, or psychomoral essence, it is of utmost importance that the person is seen as a seeker of truth, the good, and thus as a seeker of beatitude and Supreme Truth and Good. The person must be seen as such, if for no other reason, than he does have a deep and universal psychomoral (i.e., cognitive and volitional) yearning and disquietude amidst the reality of human existence.

Indeed, this deepest of human yearning and distressing disquietude is often experienced most acutely by those who have been driven by their existential condition and vicissitudes to seek formal help as therapants in regards to their essential well-being. It is these very therapants who may feel most acutely that their intrinsic incompleteness, or unrequited yearnings of their deepest desires, are not fulfillable in and of their own selves. It is these very therapants who may even be on the brink of total despair in experiencing an infinite void within the core of their being.

It is advanced that, while still factoring in the uneven vicissitudes of individual lives, many of those with discernible distress and ego-reactivity (or its sometimes disordered mental symptomology) have a higher degree of psychomoral sensitivity and thus feel most accurately the inherent lack and even wretchedness of living without a tethering to a divine Other from whom all else depends. If the desire for a fulfillment unlimited in capacity is indeed the deepest desire of the human person, then it is the duty of anyone who is directing a person psychomorally to, at the very least, help the therapant make peace with, if not fulfill, that capacity, that emptiness. It is a psychomoralitic paradox that by entering deeply into this emptiness, the remedy for essential mal-being is found.

Being, Truth & Good

Homo sapiens' specific difference as *seeker of truth and yearner for the good* necessarily makes him subject to psychomoral suffering even in—or rather *especially in*—pristine well-being. *Homo sapiens'* specific difference makes him prone to despair and a whole slew of essential mal-being maladies. Psychomoralitics thus sees essential human trauma and triumph as part and parcel of the human vocation. Indeed, psychomoralitics views essential mal-being not purely as a negative inability to bear the trauma of the human vocation, but as a pressing invitation to triumphantly embrace that vocation.

What comes from a logical, philosophical recognition of the human need for the Other (i.e., First Cause whose essence is being) is the recognition of the human person's teleology; that is, the specific difference of the human person's *qua* person. Thus the human person is made for and ordered towards truth and good, and any valid and efficacious psychomoralitic intervention must facilitate this process. What then is the relationship between truth, good, being, and Supreme Being? And what are the specific psychomoralitic ramifications of these concepts?

Thomism defines the real, the true, and the good as being (Lt., *esse).* Thomistic ontology holds that the *real*, the *true*, and the *good* all signify *being*, although from differing viewpoints. To understand the convertibility of being, the real, the true, and the good is to ground existence firmly in an objective order that is independent of man's thinking, cognitive grasp of it, or subjective wishes. Such an objective order is also a unifying principle that integrates all aspects of human experience, from spiritual yearnings to mundane calculation.

In this Thomistically explicated objective order, all derives from and hinges on Supreme Being, being whose essence is existence and therefore not caused but the prime cause of all. This Supreme Being is thus the Ultimately Real, the Ultimately True, and the Ultimately Good. Inherent in this Thomistic understanding is the ramification that the human person's final end, the very reason for human existence, is to receive the Ultimate Real, assent to the Ultimate True and possess the real and the true as the Ultimate Good, all of which is Ultimate or Supreme Being.

Being, the real, the true, and the good refer to the same entity in its analogies because an Ultimate Supreme Being necessarily is the Ultimately Real, the Ultimately True, and the Ultimately Good. For purposes of therapeutic intervention, psychomoralitics distinguishes these different aspects of being as follows:

1. Being: When some objective *being* has been receptively encountered existentially in itself, it is the *real*. This is to apprehend[57] that being (things or a thing) exists without yet naming or defining what that being specifically is.

2. Truth: As object of a mind knowing it to be as it is, a *being* is true. "Truth is the proclamation of being."[58]

3. Good: As object of a will in positive regard toward it for some perfection it is or has, a being is called good. The *good* is that which is desirable.

---

57 In an existential, experiential, and precognitive manner.

58 Hilary of Poitiers (310 – 367 A.D.).

An Existential Conceptualization

As delineated above, the psychomoralitic conceptualization is a Thomistically grounded philosophy of *being* and *existence.* This existential orientation not only allows psychomoralitics to use *the real* as the definitive measurement of essential well-being but so too makes possible psychomoralitics' efficacy. When a person acknowledges the truth that there is an Other that is the *pure unlimited act of being*, a Being that by its very nature exists and is thus the First Cause of being, he acknowledges his own creaturehood as well. Acknowledgment of one's creaturehood is acknowledging that one need not exist, but exists only through the auspices of that Other. This realization of one's own creaturely contingency is the fundamental truth about human existence and thus forms the basis of self-identity and self-knowledge, which, as will be seen, are requisite for effective psychomoralitic intervention.

Because of its basis in a philosophy of being/existence, psychomoralitics is able to unite being and essence in practice, viz., the subjective, inductive, and phenomenological, to the objective, deductive, and metaphysical. It is the subjective, inductive, and phenomenological dynamics that are crucial to both relational interaction and to a diagnostic understanding[59] while the objective, deductive, and metaphysical are crucial to establishing a normative goal of essential well-being and human flourishing.

---

59 See Chapter 12: *R.E.V.E.R.E.* p.213

In considering essential well-being as *receiving-the-real,* *assenting-to-truth,* and *choosing-the-good* a psychomoralist must take into account both the therapant's subjective experience of "the real" and objective reality itself. For a psychomoralist to acknowledge only objective reality while remaining insensitive to a therapant's subjective experience would be analogous to a physician understanding the principles of physical health while being unable to recognize the anomaly of disease. An effective psychomoralist must then be able to gain the recipient's subjective perspective (to see the world as the recipient sees it) so as to understand the specific mal-being and disorder that is entailed therein when measured against objective reality.

Induction and Deduction

In psychomoralitic inductive reasoning that begins with phenomenological observation, a psychomoralist garners knowledge by noting the therapant's particular characterological manifestations—from coping mechanisms, to deeper egoistic passions and reactivity, to deeper still psychic passions—and from these, extrapolates general diagnostic conclusions. Deductive reasoning's utilization of logical analysis applies general truths about the nature of man to the particular therapant in order to uncover the etiology of his maladies of mal-being. To this end, psychomoralitic induction begins with particular symptomology and manifestations and ends with general diagnostic categorization, while psychomoralitic deduction begins with general anthropological principles and ends with particular etiological conclusions.

Together, induction and deduction make possible the compilation of a thorough psychomoral profile. So while a completely deductive psychomoral approach would be able to present the objective ideal and goal of essential well-being, it would be unable to facilitate the therapant's attainment of that goal because it would miss the phenomenon of the person and his subjective experience. On the other hand, a completely inductive psychomoral approach (especially one based primarily on symptomology as is the case with the mental health field) does not take into account the objective nature of the human person and thus cannot systematically remedy a therapant's essential mal-being and disorders.

Any complete epistemology, clinical or not, must admit of both the inductive/phenomenological process and the deductive/logical process. Induction and deduction are two sides of the same coin and, more often than not, the epistemological process constantly fluxes between the two. The psychomoralitic theoretical conceptualization that in practice weds phenomenological existentialism[60] to deductive Thomistic metaphysics assures the

---

60 It is important to note that the danger of an existentialism without moorings in objectivity is especially grave in humanistic clinical interventions. The professionally and popularly dominant humanistic schools of mental health, such as those of Rogers or Maslow, are especially apt to exacerbate ego-reactivity and mal-being by the encouragement of radical subjectivity. The mental health professions are apt to fall into the pitfalls of an unbridled subjectivism (which feeds the

integrity of the psychomoralitic process itself. Indeed, Thomism's epistemology of conceptual realism is based on the validity of both inductive phenomenological knowledge and deductive philosophical knowledge, which together produces logical reasoning.[61] This line of logical reasoning connecting the two points of certitude (POC) can be represented thus:

Empirical Truth POC ‹‹‹‹‹‹‹‹‹‹‹›››››››› Philosophical Truth POC

Subalternation

Subalternation is the subordination of a lower science to that of a higher science when that lower science depends upon principles derived from the higher science. The new topography and spiritual intervening art that is psychomoralitics is a result of such a strict subalternation to the ontological and anthropological philosophy of Thomism. Psychomoralitics unites the empirically

---

very symptomology they seek to treat) not due to its valid recognition of the need to build therapeutic rapport, but due to its non-assent to philosophically objective truths about the human person.

61 The following logical reasoning is an example of basic syllogistic reasoning: *All humans are mortal*, (the major inductive premise), *I am a human*, (the minor inductive premise), *therefore, I am mortal*, (the deductive conclusion). But even the fact of all humans are mortal can be based on the deductive or philosophical reasoning. But then again, all authentic philosophy is essentially a philosophy of death, which means the inductive experience of death is the very catalyst for philosophy. Thus for the human person there is a constant dependent meshed interplay between the two points of human certitude.

scientific and the philosophically scientific by subalternating the empirical to the philosophical. This can also be described as integrating the qualitative with the quantitative.

As is shown above, the *nature of reality* which is explicated in *ontological* philosophy is absolutely essential to any applied psychomoral intervention. So too, as will be seen, the nature of man explicated in an anthropological philosophy is absolutely necessary for the development of an adequate underlying psychomoral topography and subsequent diagnostic accuracy and intervention efficacy.

Any applied humanistic intervening art, and most pertinently any so called clinical psychology, is not competent to philosophize on its own in this regard. Philosophy is a higher science not only because it studies the human person in a more complete and abstract manner than does applied humanistic interventions; but because it is able to study the non-empirical psychomoral realm of the human person, whereas empirical sciences cannot. For example, just as music depends on the facts of arithmetic for its composition and performance, but cannot in itself determine the principles of calculation, so does the science of any applied humanistic intervention (such as clinical psychology) depend on factual findings of philosophy for its working content, but cannot in itself determine the principles of the nonempirical nature of the real, truth, and goodness as they pertain to the human person receiving-the-real, assenting-to-truth, and choosing-the-good.

Epistemology

Once *reality* is defined, it is pertinent for philosophical psychology to understand how a person comes to know that reality. For an applied intervening humanistic science it is minimally necessary to hold that a person *can* at least know. How a person knows is the subject of epistemology. In epistemology the interplay of the material and non-material is studied. In this interplay the senses, whose organs are material instruments, convey the truth to the non-material intellect.[62]

----

62 There are two types of human knowledge. The first is that of the particular kind, which is knowledge of an individual material being through the senses. The second is that of the universal kind, which by definition is never exhausted by the being of any one of the material things of which it is predicated as its "what-it-is". Thomism holds that knowledge of the individual material beings is the actualization of the *cogitative sense* which engages sense images. Thomism further holds that because of the materiality of the particular being, this cogitative sense to be able to engage it must be material as well.

The other Thomistic component in human knowing is the immaterial abstraction of the universal. *Agent intellect* is the name of a human beings' ability to discern and thereby consider ("abstract") the universal without having to consider any *one* particular instance of it. Because the universal concept is immaterial (being common to, yet not fully identical with, any particular) Thomism holds that the agent intellect too must be immaterial to abstract it. It is then in this agent intellect that the beginnings of the immaterial appear to be. Though the agent intellect depends on the cogitative sense and its organ in order for there to be something present from which to abstract the essence, named with a universal term, still, abstracting from the sensed material particular cannot be the being in operation of a material particular such as a man's frontal lobe. In a very real sense, we do *not* think "with our brain."

It is the immaterial intellective operation that lies behind a fundamental presupposition of psychomoralitics: in his knowing, man assents to truth, the reality, or the essence of a thing. "Only a philosophy that upholds a spiritual faculty can explain even the possibility of knowledge."[63] If a person's idea of a thing that exists is not at *the* essence *of* the being that is, then that being cannot really be known, it is incomprehensible. Concepts then are merely unreliable creations of the mind. If one cannot know the true essence of a being then all that is known is a creative concept that is only a reaction to the physical sensation of such a being. Such a position leads to the rabbit hole of skepticism, and even invalidates the findings of empirical science. Such a position also does violence to common sense, where it is taken for granted that a person can indeed discern reality and can validly reflect on this reality.

The Thomistic epistemology outlined above is called *conceptual realism*. In practice, conceptual realism is the premise for everyday living; that is, that a person can intentionally and effectively interact with his environment because he can discern reality and truth via an *intellectual abstraction* whereby he knows what things exist independently of himself. Conceptual realism holds that this ability to abstract must be posited on an immaterial intellective process. It must be immaterial because thinking and truly knowing of a another being (or thing) that is *outside* of the thinker means it is *within* the thinker. That which is abstracted is the essence of the thing perceived not just a material

---

63 *Ibid.*, Sheen 1938, 139.

impression, representation, or chemical correlation. Since what is abstracted and known is not simply what the senses respond to, but rather the immaterial form, the epistemology of conceptual realism is not just empirical.[64]

Reality is thus knowable because the intellective process is incorporeal, not merely the result of a chemically active organ. To be more than just haphazard, any discipline that deals with essential human well being or its symptomology must at a minimum accept the epistemological conclusion of Thomistic conceptual realism: that *man is in essence a spiritual essence and thus reality is knowable.* Thus psychomoralitics' foundation of conceptual realism gives it the ability to have reality and reality's knowability, as the touchstone of essential human well-being and flourishing.

---

64 But nor is conceptual realism just idealistic (e.g., Platonistic), for it holds that the known form is common to, yet not fully identical with, any one particular instance, and is the nature *of* the known thing.

5. PSYCHOMORALITIC TOPOGRAPHY

THE PSYCHOMORAL REALM EXISTS. It is what every person draws upon to live life daily. It is the essence of a person's very humanity and individuality. It is the underlying realm that makes free choice possible. Yes, the psychomoral realm makes possible good or bad acts, merit or culpability, virtue or vice, indeed love or hate. Thus, from the psychomoral realm comes all truly human *qua* human acts. It is also the locus of essential well-being, ego-reactivity, and mal-being.

Thus the clear and exact topography (or mapping) of this psychomoral realm is the key to the psychomoralitic inducing of maturation, essential well-being, and human flourishing, as well as the key for the remedying of ego defensiveness and mal-being. Conversely, an erroneous or deficient understanding of the psychomoral nature of the human person will result in clinical interventions that at best are hit or miss, and at worst are impeding of maturation and well-being and exacerbating of ego defenses and mal-being. The overall failure and lack of clinical efficacy that today characterizes the mental health professions is due directly to their erroneous and/or deficient understanding of the psychomoral nature of the human person.

Psychomoralitics' topography, or mapping of the soul, is keyed on the philosophy of Thomistic psychological and moral anthropology. Psychomoralitic topography is a charting of the immaterial psychomoral realm of a person. It is within this underlying psychomoral realm that assenting to and acting upon reality takes place; that is, it is within this realm that the moral or truly human act takes place. Thus it is in this soul-deep realm where any truly transformative intervention must take place.

Though physiological factors—which by definition are not soul-deep—can be highly impacting on ego-reactivity, they are neither determinative nor etiological. Tellingly, the mental health profession's DSM does not even make the distinction between its disorders that are physiologically based and those that are strictly psychological; that is, between organic brain disorders and those classifications of symptom constellations that have an inorganic etiology. This glaring lack of discrimination is due to the DSM's non-recognition of the psychomoral realm that is the determinative and etiological locus of all non-organic symptomology. Again, it is this exclusion and subsequent non-awareness of the psychomoral realm and its topography that produces the generally ineffectual, and often gravely harmful, results of the mental health professions' treatments.

Psychomoralitics' Anthropological Foundation

The psychomoralitic topography is derived from a Thomistic psychological and moral anthropology that stands alone in its historical, academic, commonsensical, and now humanistic clinical application. This Thomistic anthropology is confirmed historically by being part and parcel of a philosophical corpus incomparable in its ancient origins, unbroken continuity, and ever new applicability. It is an anthropology confirmed academically by a scholarship that is matchless in both depth and breadth of output and integral development. It is an anthropology confirmed commonsensically in resonance with the experience and sensibilities of the average person and universal consensus. It is now an anthropology confirmed clinically by a plethora of psychomoralitic anecdotal case study data that promises further empirical validation of an unprecedented efficacy.[65]

The translation of the philosophy of Thomistic psychological and moral anthropology into the psychomoralitic topography makes for a ready and efficacious clinical application. Any conceptual application, and specifically one that claims to be essentially humanistic and clinical, should be a simplification of its underlying theory; for again such an application is a lower science that is properly subalternated to the science of anthropology or philosophy of human nature. So too, a theory, no matter how complex, is validated by its ability to be simplified down to the commonsensical and obvious. This is because a theory that is true will have real life, practical, and even simple applications. Such is the case with psychomoralitics' subalternation to, and simplified application of, Thomistic anthropology.

---

65 See http://www.psychomoral.com/testimonies.html.

When an explicit anthropology and/or topography does exist in the mishmash of the many mental health theories, it is *created* to support the clinical conceptualization, which itself is a creative narrative given to clinical observation and/or symptomology. This is the inverse order of a lower science determining a higher one. This is the case in behavioral and biological mental health conceptualizations, where, respectively, either overt behaviors or symptoms are the premise for the ensuing theoretical conceptualizations. Nor are the classical personality theories derived from or subalternated to a fuller, more elaborate, and guiding anthropology. Rather these personality theories *are the* anthropology, and are a creative interpretation given to clinical observation.

As has been noted, the biological mental health nosologies are based on symptomology. That is, the biological conceptualization of mental health and disorder is made up of theories fabricated to fit symptomology. For instance, in the prevalent theory of depression, the narrative is that a lack of the neurotransmitter serotonin within the synapses causes depression. This narrative was fabricated in accord with the observation that depressive symptomology was sometimes alleviated by a psychotropic drug (*Selective Serotonin Re-Uptake Inhibitors* or *SSRI's*) that was itself theorized to increase serotonin within the synapses. But just because a drug may relieve symptomology does not mean that symptomology was caused by a deficiency in that drug, just as a lack of *acetylsalicylic acid* (i.e., *aspirin*) *does not cause* headaches, though its presence may alleviate symptomology.

Personality theories are what comes closest to an actual philosophical anthropology in the mental health professions. Here the personality theory is created to fit manifestations of perceived symptomatic psychopathology. But such contrived personality theories cannot stand on their own and cannot be the higher directive science of a subalternated clinical application. Rather a personality theory is subordinated to the clinical conceptualization because it derives from it. While personality theories, and the biological basis theories, may be built upon some valid but superficial empirical observations, it is because of their being contrived from these observations that they entail an inbred circular reasoning. Enclosed in such tautological reasoning, these conceptualizations can have no guiding subalternating principles and are thus rendered insusceptible to external validation.

The simplicity of a clinical conceptualization and application is not only an indicator that it is based on a valid and adequate anthropology, but it is a harbinger of efficacious intervention as well. A relatively simple clinical conceptualization both facilitates use by practitioners and, even more importantly, facilitates use by the therapants themselves; who, after all, are the one's who must master the conceptualization and its application for it to be truly efficacious.

Ludicrous Mental Health Theories

The creative genius of the personality theorists and the technological wizardry of the pharmacological industry are impressive. But as elaborate as the personality theories may be, they are mere tripe in comparison to the wisdom of the ages, nor can the increasing prescription of increasingly powerful psychotropics mask the disorientation resulting from the loss of that wisdom. How does the correct understanding of the psychomoral realm derived from this wisdom impact the treatment of ego-reactivity and its sometimes concomitant symptomatic mental disorders? One might as well ask, how does the correct understanding of the internal combustion engine impact car mechanics?

> Imagine taking your car to a mechanic because the engine is misfiring badly. The mechanic is clad in clean blue overalls in his well lit cement floored garage. He pulls his large red tool chest over, opens the hood of your car, and whips out a shiny chrome wrench. The mechanic proceeds to display great dexterity and competency as he tinkers with the engine of your car. You even hear some changes in the engine, as he revs it up some. Impressed you ask,
>
> > *"So do you think it has to do with the spark plugs?"*
>
> He looks away from his tweaking of the engine for a second, and says,

"Excuse me?"

You repeat,

"The spark plugs, I was wondering if they may be the problem."

Already back at his work he looks at you askance, and with some impatience asks,

"The what plugs?"

You stutter,

"Spark...spark plugs."

He stands up straight and impatiently puts his screwdriver down. Looking at you suspiciously, he asks,

"What on God's green earth on you talking about?"

You begin to become hesitant as the mechanic picks up his shiny silver crescent wrench and fingers its variable adjustment with expertise, but nonetheless you say,

"Ah...you know sparks...gas fumes... internal combustion engine."

Your car is relatively new and you even begin wondering if they still use internal combustion engines. The mechanic looks at you with professional disdain, and maybe feeling a little threatened, spits out,

> *"Eternal discombobulation! What the %&$@#%^ are talking about?!?" I'm just trying to fix these nuts and bolts of your car."*

That's it, you're out of there, if nothing more than because of his rudeness. So you meekly ask him,

> *"Do you think it will drive the twenty some miles to arrive home without a problem?"*

He looks at you like you have totally lost your mind,

> *"I'm a mechanic! I don't know nothing about drive, arrive, man-alive! I'm just trying make this here noise maker sound better."*

Resisting the temptation to utter your own incredulous expletive, you give him a twenty and do actually *drive-off*. But the mechanic does not seem to have noticed, for he is diligently wiping off his tools waiting for the next bolt or screw to adjust on the sound and fume producing units.

As absurd as this scenario is, its equivalent is being played out daily in mental health clinics around the world. For the internal psychomoral dynamics, etiology, and teleology of the human being is something that the mental health profession is ludicrously unaware of. But without a proper understanding of the psychomoral realm, effective treatment of most of the mental health profession's designated symptomatic disorders is haphazard at best. At worst, these mental health treatments are lethal to a person's psychomoral well-being.

Perennial Philosophical Anthropology

Whereas the mental health field fundamentally rejects, or is unaware or unappreciative of the psychomoral realm, psychomoralitics does not eschew any truths, be they of the empirical or philosophical sciences. This is because psychomoralitics is based on a Thomism that is integrative of all truth.

> [Thomistic] principles are, in a sense, the same as those of apparently different, and sometimes opposed, philosophies—with this difference only: that in Thomism these principles are taken in the fullness of their meaning.. . . *All that is true in any other philosophy can be justified by the principles of Thomas Aquinas, and there is no other philosophy that it is possible to profess without having to ignore, or to reject, some conclusions that are true in the light of these principles.* Speaking in a more familiar way, one can be a Thomist without losing the truth of any other philosophy, whereas one cannot ascribe to any other philosophy without losing some of the truth available to the disciple of Thomas Aquinas.[66]

Some other "philosophies" are indeed open to all and sundry truths because they lack any internal coherence or are undefined and ambiguous, and therefore, these are more aptly pseudo-

---

66 Gilson, Etienne. 1960. *Elements of Christian Philosophy.* Garden City, NY: Doubleday. p.278.

philosophies, that is, pseudo-sciences. Other philosophies have an internal coherence similar to Thomism, but that very coherence shuts them off from truths outside their philosophical system. Thomism by the very fact of its unique internal consistency and unity is open to all truths and able to incorporate them into its philosophical system. Thus psychomoralitics is enabled by its Thomistic nature to perfect that which is true and useful in the empirical psychological sciences by incorporating them into its own integral conceptualization.

But ultimately what assures the superiority of what has been dubbed the "perennial philosophy"[67] may well depend on it being the initial philosophical conceptualization, beginning with the ancient Greeks and brought to perfection in Thomism. It is as if it is the very freshness of this ancient encounter of philosophizing man with reality that accounts for the (conceptual) realism and clarity that characterizes it. This first systematized philosophical conceptualization was the springboard for the subsequent derivative philosophies that proliferated after the Thomistic apex. But these subsequent philosophies seem to suffer from a neurotic over-thinking and a jaded skepticism that lacks the newness,

---

67 "Perennial Philosophy: the philosophical tradition of the world's great thinkers from Plato, Aristotle, and Aquinas to their modern successors dealing with problems of ultimate reality (as the nature of being) and sometimes emphasizing mysticism as opposed to skepticism." (*Merriam-Webster's Dictionary*). Such a so-called "mysticism" remains open to realities that are not fully grasped by the human intellect, whereas skepticism is closed-off to those realities.

moral rectitude, and rock solid commonsense that is present in the Thomistic philosophical encounter. Accordingly, psychomoralitics poises its practitioners to encounter each individual therapant with this same newness, moral rectitude, and rock solid commonsense.

Psychomoral Elements

The following explication of the psychomoral topography has been developed from Thomistic philosophical anthropology so as to be precisely applicable to an essential humanistic, specifically psychomoral, intervention. Though a deeper philosophical understanding may be helpful to a psychomoralitic practitioner, the topographical formulation herein suffices for an essential humanistic intervention. As per the principle of subalternation, just as the concert pianist need not be a mathematician to play mathematically based music, the psychomoral practitioner need not be a Thomistic meta-physician to implement a metaphysically based psychomoralitic intervention.

For purposes of intervening to facilitate essential well-being and remedy mal-being and ego-reactivity, the topography of the psychomoral realm can be considered as six primary elements: *psyche, ego, psyche passions, ego passions, coping mechanisms,* and *avenues of approach.* Although the topographical elements and the dynamics therein are described somewhat materially they are of a psychomoral and thus immaterial nature. So too, though psychomoralitics' use of terms such as *psyche* or *ego* has been used in the mental health disciplines, these terms have their origins in the ancient Western world's anthropological tradition. Though these terms may be understood in various ways by other humanistic intervening disciplines, in psychomoralitics they correspond directly to, or are derived, from their original conceptualization.

Psyche

In the *psyche* (Gk., *soul*) is found the true essence of the human person. This psyche is the ultimate perfecting form of that portion of organic matter that together with the psyche (i.e., hylomorphic composition) comprises an individual human being. The human psyche has tripartite faculties. These faculties are categorized, from lowest to highest, as either vegetative, sensitive, or rational. It is from the rational faculties that comes the specific difference of the human person: that of an enfleshed being that has reason and freewill. The psyche and its highest rational faculty can be obscured, debilitated, and bound by the ego and its passions and coping mechanisms, which in turn can likewise be triggered by the vegetative and sensitive faculties.

The path of maturation and psychomoral well-being entails the psyche increasing in its receptivity, assent to, and choosing of reality in both breadth and depth. This requires that the psyche be unencumbered by a dominant ego in its subjective and reality rejecting orientation. From the highest faculty of the psyche comes the ability to rationally choose and fully accept objective reality even when that reality is not in accord with or threatens harm to the subjective good of the ego. But so too, it is the psyche that can choose to acquiesce to the ego and allow the domination of the ego's defenses, thus choosing a lower subjective good of the ego over the objective good. The crucial psychomoralitic point is at this juncture of choice between the objective higher good and the subjective egoistic good. The intensity of this psychomoralitic point is determined by the degree that the choice entails the attainment of either the objective good or the subjective good to the detriment of the other.

Ego

The *ego* (Lt., *I*)[68] is part of a person, but it is not an essential part. The ego is in essence an apostatizing pride and subjective self-love. The variable part of the ego is its particular defenses, *viz.*, coping mechanisms and passions, and the unique combinations thereof. The ego *et al.* is that which is abnegated and transcended in effective psychomoralitics. The ego exists due to the psychomoral turning from the truth and good of objective reality in favor of lower truths and goods of subjective self-interest.[69]

---

68 In psychomoralitics, *ego* translates as not only *I*, but as *me, myself, and I.*

69 The former *turning from,* or *apostatizing,* is conceptualized in Thomism as the phenomenon of pride, and the latter *turning to* subjective self-interest conceptualized as self-love.

When choices are made in favor of lower subjective goods over higher objective goods then the ego hampers the psyche in its objective use of reason and volition, and indeed marshals this reason and volition to its own subjective use. Choosing subjective self-interest to the detriment or exclusion of objective reality is a psychomoral act that utilizes defenses to preserve or increase the ego. The ego's hampering of the psyche is done via ego passions and coping mechanisms, though the actual egoistic or apostatizing act is a rational free choice.

Passions

Passions are physical manifestations that have their origins in the impact of reality upon the ego and the psyche. Though the passions have their origins in the psychomoral realm, they can be experienced in the body as physically felt emotions ("emotions" being mere physical sensations). Due to the person's hylomorphic nature, all passions have a physical manifestation,[70] but can range from the intensely visceral to the subtly spiritual.

All passions are brought about by impacting reality, be it negative or positive stimulus. As physical emotions are brought about by either the negative stimuli of physical pain or the positive stimuli of physical pleasure, psychomoral passions are brought about by either the negative stimuli of psychic "pain" or

---

70 The physiology of emotion is closely linked to arousal of the nervous system with various states and strengths of arousal relating to particular passions.

the positive stimuli of psychic "pleasure." Psychomoral passions of the ego are brought about by either the negative stimuli of humiliation or the positive stimuli of aggrandizement. Psychomoral passions of the psyche are brought about by either the negative stimuli of sorrow or the positive stimuli of joy. The same impacting reality or stimuli can cause different and even conflicting passions and emotions to be elicited from the three elements of body, ego, and psyche.

Coping Mechanisms

The coping realm is where a person keeps the psychomoral passions in check and deals with impacting reality in an ego enhancing manner. In coping, a person is selectively open to reality. This selectivity is where the myriad of choices are made that either lead to a gradual increased openness to impacting reality and hence maturation and well-being or to a gradual blunting of impacting reality and the risk of ego passion reactivity when that reality can no longer be blunted.

Coping mechanisms are ego generated but are not as binding of the intellect and will as when the ego passions are dominant. Coping mechanisms admit of the ability to reflect upon oneself with some objectivity even if for a non-objectively good end.[71] That which threatens harm to the ego is defended against or

_____

71 Thus a person may appear more egocentric or even vicious because of an organic inability to so reflect, as per a lack of social prosody. This can also be caused or exacerbated by a deeper than normal degree of openness to reality and hence manifestation of the psyche.

acceded to in various ways that manifest themselves in both abiding character and relatively tenuous personality. Coping mechanisms become firmly established as a person ages and is habituated in defending the ego in certain ways. The coping mechanisms protect the ego from full reality by obscuring, distorting, or not recognizing aspects of reality. A habituated coping should be seen as a state where mal-being and ego passions are not remarkably present, but not as the state of well-being itself. While paradoxically the coping state may facilitate a certain level of functionality, it is nonetheless the psychomoralitic doldrums, a static state that does not admit of maturation and its concomitant increase of well-being.

Avenues of Approach

Avenues of approach are both openings outward to reality and openings inward to the essence of a person. They are thus two-way, both giving a person clearer sight of reality and affording a clearer manifestation of his authentic person as well. Avenues of approach are highly interrelated with coping mechanisms and ego passions. As strengths can become weaknesses and weaknesses strengths, so too can ego defenses become avenues of approach.

When a person is pierced by a particularly painful impacting reality he may create a coping mechanism or experience a dominant ego passion against it. But so too when a person has a particular coping mechanism or ego passion against a particularly painful impacting reality, he may create an avenue of approach in its place. This latter creation of an avenue of approach in place of a coping mechanism and/or dominant ego passion is of the essence of the psychomoralitic process. Avenues of approach are created when the negative impacting reality of humiliation against the ego is receptively accepted by the psyche's reason and will, thus not allowing the ego defenses, be they coping mechanisms or passions, to interfere.

Other Psychomoral Groupings

As practical designations to facilitate the conveyance of the psychomoral conceptualization and its psychomoralitic application, the six psychomoral elements may be grouped into *pseudo-self, character,* and *personality.* The pseudo-self is the combined complex of the ego, its passions, and coping mechanisms. As a whole the pseudo-self is the object of psychomoralitic abnegation. Most often a person, at least those of the technarcistic bent, identifies the pseudo-self with his essential self. However, it is the subjugation and reduction of the pseudo-self that brings out the essential and authentic self of the psyche. The recognition of the pseudo-self and its egoistic essence as distinct from authentic self and its psychic essence is crucial to effective psychomoralitics.

Character is the unique combination of an individual's psychomoral habits; as per his specific set of coping mechanisms, predominate ego passions, and avenues of approach. Dispositions also add to character as less habituated qualities. Character develops via psychomoral acts and abides even in the presence of cognitive trauma or decline. Psychomoralitics' aim is to effect deep characterological change.

Personality is the overall *presentation* of the person. The more authentic a person is, the more the personality ceases to act as veneer but rather both diminishes and manifests the character unimpeded by coping mechanisms. Personality is influenced by aptitudes and inaptitudes, physiological dispositions (especially neurological), and external relational and social factors. Personality is relatively tenuous as compared to character and can be temporarily altered by an inability to cope with stressors and permanently altered by cognitive trauma or decline, in which case the underlying character is made manifest.

The more receptive and authentic a person is the less they are able to be put into so called personality categories, be it in accord with modern psychological classifications such as *Meyers-Briggs* or simplistic poetical categories such as the ancient temperaments. A psychomorally sound person responds prudently to a situation, that is, responds not in accord with his subjective disposition but in accord with the truth of the situation.

6. Openness to Reality

THE REALITY-BASED PSYCHOMORALITIC CONCEPTUALIZATION of essential human well-being and flourishing as per receiving-the-real, assenting-to-truth, and choosing-the-good involves the dynamic interaction of psychomoral elements in relationship to reality and to each other, all of which together culminate in the sum of a person's openness to reality. As delineated in the psychomoral topography, what comes into play specifically are the elements of psyche, ego, passions, coping mechanisms, and avenues of approach.

For psychomoral well-being the psyche must be dominant, for it is both the essential source of a person's rationality and volition and, as such, that which encounters reality in a purely objective manner. Each choice a person makes while utilizing the elements of the psychomoral realm is either moral, immoral, or amoral. A moral act would, at minimum, not diminish a person's openness to reality and would have the ego's subjective good reciprocal with the psyche's objective good.

The moral act will increase rectitude as it entails an abnegation of the ego, that is, as it entails a love greater than self-love. Such an act is also a psychomoralitic act, or ego caustic act. Such a moral and psychomoralitic act entails a volitional receptivity to impacting reality that abnegates the ego. Here the moral act entails an objective loss of a lower good in favor of a higher one, thus forgoing a less sorrowful but myopic *coping* in favor of an openness to a wider reality and an ensuing deeper sorrow, and joy as well.

The cognitive and volitional faculties are specifically that which make the human person human and thus constitute the elements of the psychomoral and fully human act. The mental health field with its reductionistic and/or erroneous anthropology tends to diminish or all together exclude free will, especially when its symptomatic mental disordering is diagnosed. Psychomoralitics, with its foundation of Thomistically defined cognitive and volitional faculties, insures the inclusion and primacy of human free will, and seeks only to increase that free will and ensue a moral culpability.

As will be seen, the mere presence of symptomatic mental disordering does not exclude volition as an etiological factor, but to the contrary indicates that volition is indeed being challenged. The psychomoral human act entails an openness to reality and the elements of receiving-the-real, assenting-to-truth, and choosing-the-good; that is, it entails all a person *qua* person's faculties. Thus the ability to so act constitutes the very human difference and is the basis of psychomoralitics as well.

Choosing the Higher Good

Both an increased openness to reality, that is, the creation of avenues of approach, and an increased closedness-to-reality, that is, the creation of defenses, depend on the rational, volitional psychomoral act of receiving-the-real, assenting-to-truth, and choosing-the-good. This act culminates in a person's either choosing a higher good over a lower good in accord with objectivity or choosing a lower good over a higher good in accord with ego subjectivity. When the psychomoral choice is in accord with objectivity and entails the sacrifice of an ego subjective good the result is the enhancement or creation of avenues of approach. When the psychomoral choice is in accord with subjectivity and entails the sacrifice of an objective good the result is the enhancement or creation of ego defenses.

Psychomoralitics then recognizes a hierarchy of reality, of the real, the truth, and the good. The will's object, or the final end of the psychomoral act, is necessarily always a good; however, the good it chooses is not necessarily the higher good or the good it should seek. In an act that is ego enhancing, a person, in accord with a subjective appraisal, chooses a lower good even though it excludes or destroys a higher good. That lower good, though objectively inferior to the superior good, is chosen because subjectively it is held by the ego to be more beneficial. Thus to a greater or lesser extent, the ego in its subjective desires binds the psyche, distorts reality, and orders volition to its own ends. The proper psychomoral act, conversely, is where a person, in accord with an objective appraisal, sacrifices a lower good for a higher good, even though such a choice may be detrimental to the ego.

In that man is a physical being, he has urgent physical needs that call for attainment of their fulfilling goods. But as urgent as these physical needs may be, this does not mean these fulfilling goods are the highest goods. Though these needs are his sole concern in infancy, as a person grows in psychomoral maturation he assents to the fact that aspects of the real, truth, and good transcend his existence. Indeed, in mature wisdom a person realizes that the attainment of the physical goods is but transitory and never secure. A psychomorally mature person comes to understand and accept his radical physical vulnerability. Furthermore, a person advanced in essential well-being not only accepts his physical vulnerability but orders the physical unto higher transcendental goods, even unto physical death.

While seeking to maintain life, a mature person of essential well-being recognizes the inevitability of death and of goods that are higher than his physical preservation, and thus would not do whatever it takes to preserve his life. Neither can the person relegated to fighting solely for his substance or life, nor the person obsessively afraid of the losing his life (or security), ever reach full human maturation which entails freely giving one's life in service or sacrifice to the highest goods. This freely given life may be the mere acceptance of the truth of an impending death or it may be the sacrificial choice to march into the very jaws of death for a higher good than one's existence.

For the human person, physical suffering and death entails an even deeper and more painful suffering than the physical. Physical suffering entails a psychomoral suffering, both an egoistic humiliation and a psychic sorrow. Indeed, death is the greatest humiliation, where a person is stripped of all.[72]

Teleology is a being's purpose or end. As previously explained,[73] the human person's purpose is to seek truth. Teleology of a human being *qua* being is mere existence. But teleology of a human being *qua* human involves reason, and thus the seeking of wisdom; for that is *homo sapiens'* (Lt., *sapientia* – wisdom) specific difference and hence specific end. The preservation of life which the human person has in common with all living beings is a fundamental good. But because it is only a fundamental, basic foundational, or lower good, it necessarily admits of higher goods. The psychomorally mature person realizes that he can and should be willing to sacrifice a lower good to preserve or attain a higher good. This maturation is the hallmark of both wisdom and essential well-being. Thus, to prudently discern authentic higher goods—and not mere subjective goods that the ego may present—one must be receptive to the fullness of reality, assent to the objective truth, and be willing to choose the highest of goods.

---

72 Beware therefore of the medical and mental health professions' preaching of the oxymoron "dying with dignity." There is no dignity in dying, unless by dignity is meant a drugged reductionistic stupor state that replaces the ultimate drama of life/death with a smothering narcotic bliss.

73 See Chapter 4: § *Being, Truth & Good*. p.74

Psychomoral Rectitude

When a person chooses to fulfill a need or acquire a good that destroys a higher need or good, such an act is deemed disordered or immoral. Indeed, a person is called to forgo lower goods in pursuit of higher goods; this is the essence of nobility and heroism; it is the essence of the truly human life. Although the human person needs to have life and sustenance to function, his functioning should not be ordered to sustaining biological life. The tautological belief that the full meaning of biological existence is biological existence itself, can but produce a superficial coping, a looming disordered ego-reactivity, a philosophical vortex of absurdity and nihilism, and a final inexorable despair.

The will depends on the intellect for its object of volition or teleological goal or good. The intellect presents the truth to the will as a good (again truth and good are but differing points of view concerning being). However, even though the will depends upon the intellect to present the object to it as good, once the good is willed, the will can in turn influence the intellect by directing it toward further acquirement of the good or truth, or away from truth, even distorting the intellect's conception of the truth. Such a distortion is intellectual falsity and may be found in a faulty logic that rationalizes evil, or in the ideological raising of a lower good or truth over a higher one, or in the dismissal of a higher truth or good completely. This is why psychomoralitics is concerned not only with the intellect (or the mere *mentation* of the *mental* health field) but with the will and its freedom from the egoistic fetters, for the will is necessary for full acquirement of truth's good and can even cause the intellect to distort its concept of truth. It is the defensive exclusion of some aspects of the real, the truth, and the good that is the essence of coping, it is the distortion of the real, the truth, and the good that is the essence of ego-reactivity, and it is the fully cognizant rejection of the real, the truth, and the good that is of the essence of mal-being.

A person's psychomoral state depends on whether or not he is disposed or habituated toward receiving-the-real, assenting-to-truth, and choosing-the-good. Psychomoral rectitude is when a person's will and passions are disposed in accordance with right reason. Thus, when the volitional faculty is choosing-the-good in the steadfast service of receiving-the-real and assenting-to-truth, a person being habituated toward the true and good possesses psychomoral rectitude. Psychomoralitic virtue[74] is synonymous with habitual avenues of approach, whereas its contrary vice is synonymous with habitual ego defenses.

A person can reject the general good in view by focusing on a lesser aspect of it (that is, on a particular lower good to the exclusion of a higher good), and if this is done habitually, it can actually impair his view of that good and thus diminish his receiving-the-real. While a person's cognitive assenting-to-the-truth is not always a product of volition or moral choices (i.e., there may be organic abnormalities), his psychomoral state is

---

74 See Chapter 9: § *Beyond Virtue & Vice.* p.160

always based on cognitive assent and volition, no matter how limited that assent and volition may be. A psychomoralitic practitioner helps a therapant increase this assent and volition, that is, increase psychomoral culpability, first by facilitating individual acts toward choosing-the-good. The culmination of these individual acts eventually develops a greater dispositional, and then habitual, choosing-the-good.

Again, when being is spoken of as an object of the intellect it is called reality; when it is spoken of as an object of the will it is called the good. When the intellect's understanding coincides with reality a person possesses truth. When the will's object coincides with an objective good a person possesses the good. A person matures and opens himself up to reality when he chooses objective goods that countermand his subjective good or good of his ego. Being virtuous in a psychomoral sense then consists in being responsive to and acting in accord with reality in a sacrificial manner. For a true moral choice necessarily entails sacrificing one good for another.

Psychomoral rectitude is thus dependent on objective reality, just as the will is dependent on reason. But whether a person is virtuously open to reality or viciously closed-off does not depend on simply following a set of rules, indeed, it at times may mean breaking conventional rules. Nor, as will be seen,[75] is it the state of coping which, although being absent of manifest ego-reactivity (and possibly major symptomatic mental disordering), may

---

75 Chapter 8: *Egoistic Coping*. p.139

nonetheless be a state that is less open-to-reality than the state of ego-reactivity, and is often further ensconced in mal-being.

The Three Stages of the Psychomoral Act

Psychomoralitics is reality based—that is, *being* based—both in its ontological conceptualization that hinges on being, truth, and good and in its application where a therapant's relation to reality is the touchstone of intervention. Psychomoralitics integrates this ontology and applied intervention in the delineation of three stages of the psychomoral act. The first stage is the *existential,* which entails a therapant's interaction with being as *receiving-the-real.* This *receiving-the-real* is a precognitive and universal encounter with the real as non-particularized being-as-such. The second stage is the *cognitive,* which entails a therapant's interaction with being as an *assenting-to-truth.* This assenting-to-truth is a cognitive acceptance of being as a specific or particularized being. The third stage is the *volitional,* which entails a therapant's interaction with being as a *choosing-the-good.* This choosing-the-good is a volitional embrace of being as the good.

Receiving-the-Real

The first stage in the psychomoral is receiving-the-real. Receiving-the-real is the prerequisite existential disposition where the subconscious of the therapant is open to universal reality or *being-as-such.* Being-as-such is *encountered* precognitively rather than *assented* to cognitively (which takes place in the next stage of the psychomoral act). This is because, in cognitive assent to truth, a particularization of being and a particular truth is the object, but in existential encounter, being-as-such is the non-particularized, amorphous object. The first stage of existential receiving-the-real is to the second stage of cognitive assenting-to-the-truth as opening the eyes is to vision. Receiving-the-real, to being-as-such, is thus the prerequisite existential disposition that is required if a person is to gain an integral and objective assenting-to-the-truth.

This first stage of the existential precognitive encounter comes into play initially when the mind as a *tabula rasa* is acted upon by reality. Receiving-the-real takes place on the precognitive or subconscious level because "a mutual correlation between being and mind exists already prior to any actual perception [or] activity of the mind".[76] Note well that reality emanates from the object known, not the knowing mind. Reality in itself is oriented toward man's perceiving mind, without the mind's contribution, and simply by virtue of its very *being*, which man has not bestowed upon it. As such, from the beginning reality as receiving-the-real, and subsequently as assenting-to-truth, is objective as opposed to subjective.

Encountering reality is a passive receptivity to non particularized being-as-such. It is the facilitation of this encountering that is the psychomoralitic emphasis in the precognitive, pre-volitional stage of the subconscious. If reason

76 Pieper 1989, 62.

and volition are involved in the encountering they are involved precedently by assenting to the truth that they should be open to reality and hence choosing not to exert the will against it. In short, such a receptivity involves the all important psychomoralitic *yes*. Such an assent and choosing renders a person receptive-to-reality.

This receiving-the-real requires a positive dispositional openness to or encountering of reality and must be ever waxing through life if a person is to optimize psychomoral well-being and maturation. Thomism holds that "the spirit-based self, ordered as it is toward the whole of reality, is in its very essence called to face with an attitude of receptive, unbiased openness this universality of its world".[77] Aquinas demarcates the three levels of receiving-the-real that are possible for the human person. The first concerns only the body. The second concerns all material objects accessible through the senses. The third is directed toward being-as-such "not only toward all material things, but toward all that exists".[78]

It is this third level that transcends subjectivity and assures objectivity, which is essential for the psychomoralitic process and psychomoral well-being. It is the encounter with being-as-such that affords a person an objective perspective in which to view particular beings, oneself especially, as contingent manifestations of being-as-such or transcendent Supreme Being. Such a receptive openness requires that a person overcome the fears and

77 Pieper 1989, 98.

78 *Summa Theologica*, I, q.78.

subsequent personality defenses that shelter one from transcendent being, and that prevent one from realizing one's own radically contingent being. Choosing at the third level also entails the choosing of higher truths and goods over lower truths and goods.

Assenting-to-Truth

Poised on an existential receiving-the-real, a person is oriented to cognitive assent to particularized being, which takes place in the next stage of the psychomoral act. To the degree that a person in the first stage is existentially open and receiving-the-real he is objectively and fully assenting-to-the-truth in the second. Whereas *encountering* reality is a passive receptivity to non-particularized being-as-such, *assent* to the truth is a positive assent of the reason to a particular truth.

Truth is the cognition of that which exists: *it is being proclaimed in a particularized manner.* When in the first stage of receiving-the-real there is full receptivity, including the spiritual or transcendental (Aquinas's level of existential awareness), then a person in the second stage of cognitive assenting-to-the-truth will have an objective orientation and transcend subjectivism. This objective orientation is essential to psychomoral well-being because it allows a person to stand outside his subjective pseudo-self and so evaluate his passions, cognitions, and actions. This objective orientation is what poises a therapant to begin the psychomoralitic process of ego-abnegation and increased openness to reality.

Still, the subordination of subjectivity to objectivity does not automatically entail full assenting-to-the-truth. Once a person's receiving-the-real and objectivity is established, the truth must be brought into sight so that it can be assented to. A person may be unaware of truths, may hold erroneous tenants, or may be closed-off to some truths in an inordinate focus upon certain particular truths. Being unaware of the truth or holding erroneous tenants is a result of ignorance. Ignorance is rectified in the stage of assenting-to-the-truth through psychotherapeutic pedagogy. The psychomoralitic intervention required to rectify ignorance of the truth is *convincing*.

Whereas being unaware of the truth is the result of ignorance, being *closed-off* to the truth is the result of ego defenses. Ego defenses are formed by habitually assenting to subjective half-truths or distorted truths and choosing their subjective goods to the detriment of fuller truths and objectively higher goods. An adult person's impaired assenting-to-the-truth is rarely a result only of ignorance but entails ego defenses as well. However ignorance facilitates the creation of ego defenses and ego defenses facilitate ignorance.

Fully cognizant disordered choices of lower subjective goods to the destruction—not just exclusion—of higher objective goods are culpable acts that are vicious. When such volitional acts are habitual they form ego defenses that are categorized as vice. But not all people afflicted with vicious defense mechanisms are responsible for the full extent of that vice, for some have their assenting-to-the-truth impaired by being exposed to the vice of others. In this they form ego defenses to protect themselves from the viciousness of others and in doing so may even develop similarly vicious defenses. Thus the phenomenon of an erstwhile victim becoming a perpetrator. As such, the impairment of the assenting-to-the-truth by vice is best called *vice-effect*,[79] which does not entail determining degrees of culpability.

Vice-effect does, however, create a disposition that can sway a person toward making vicious choices himself. This is similar to the natural disposition toward vice that Aquinas calls an *inherited concupiscence*.[80] Concupiscence is the tendency to seek "creature comforts" over arduous endeavors, pleasure over pain, and is a principle that even a strict material behaviorism depends upon in its therapeutic conceptualization. It is the subjective seeking of ego pleasure/gratification or the avoidance of ego pain/humiliation to the detriment of reality that is the essence of all mal-being, ego reactivity, and symptomatic mental disordering. Whereas it is the habitual assent to truth and choosing it as the good no matter how mortifying it is to one's subjective good and ego that is the true mark of psychomoral well-being.

---

79 See Chapter 9: § *Inherited Dispositional Defect*. p.166 Also see *Imago Dei Psychotherapy, ibid.,* Chapter 8: § *Vice, Vice-Effect, & Inherited Concupiscence,* pg. 127.

80 *Summa Theologica* I-II, q. 82, a. 1.

Choosing-the-Good

Choosing-the-good is the third[81] stage of the psychomoral act and the final determining element involved in the psychomoralitic process. Whereas the existential key to essential well-being is receiving-the-real and cognitively assenting-to-the-truth, the key volitionally is choosing-the-good. In choosing-the-good the essential psychomoral act, and thus the psychomoralitic process, is not best characterized as an *exertion of the will*, if by exertion is connoted a "pulling of oneself up by the boot straps." While such an exertion of the will can indeed be laudable it is not the specific difference of true psychomoralitic transformation. Indeed, those with unbridled ego reactivity find themselves wanting in the ability to implement such a volitional exertion.

In the psychomoralitic process the use of the will is first and foremost the existential choice to not exert itself against that which does harm to the ego; that is, to letting down ego defenses. The psychomoralitic aim in volitional choice, or choosing-the-

81 Though not of immediate psychomoralitic import, Thomistically there are two steps that bridge assenting-to-the-truth and choosing-the-good. They are simple-willing and voice-of-the-primordial-conscience. Neither are areas of therapeutic intervention since they are not subject to impairment. The first step, simple-willing, cannot be impaired because of the unavoidable attraction and love of a good once it is sighted. The second step, voice-of-the-primordial-conscience (*synderesis*), cannot be impaired because this voice is always imperative, always demands that good be done and evil avoided. However, if the assenting-to-the-truth is impaired a detrimental good whose attainment destroys a greater good may present itself to these steps to the exclusion of that greater good.

good, is to *receptively* allow impacting reality to breach the defenses, abnegate the ego, and pierce into the depths of the psyche. Once so pierced, an *exertive* choice may be made from the depths of the psyche but only after a *receptive* choice is made. It is this receptive choice that is essential. Indeed, properly a prudent exertive choice or response is a fruit of the receptive choice.

The three stages of the psychomoral act — existential receiving-the-real, cognitive assenting-to-truth, and volitional choosing-the-good — are also the three stages in which the psychomoralitic process takes place. Though these three stages sequentially presuppose one another they are circularly looped. All of these psychomoral responses to reality play one upon another in various combinations. Thus a person's receptivity to universal being (or being-as-such) is the prerequisite disposition for the second stage of specific assenting-to-the-truth. A person may or may not assent to a particular truth and any assent requires some receptivity to universal being, with the greater the receptivity the greater the assent to truth. Once the second stage of the assenting-to-the-truth has been entered into, the third stage can occur where that truth is presented to the will as a good to be attained. In the third stage the will may or may not choose the good because of the pain and humiliation it entails or the pleasure and gratification it forgoes.

A Continuous Psychomoral Loop

Once the three stages of the psychomoral act have been entered into, the third loops back to the first. The second stage of cognitive assent and the third stage of volitional choice of a particular objective truth and good over subjective goods also increases the first stage's existential receptivity to universal reality and being-as-such. Adversely, not cognitively assenting to a particular truth and/or choosing it as a particular good over a subjective good impedes receiving-the-real. So too, in the second stage, the cognitively assented to principle that a person should be open to universal reality chosen as a particular good facilitates the first stage's actual existential openness to universal being. So though the existential experiencing of abnegating reality takes place first, it is the cognitive assent to the truth that this abnegation of the ego is good that enhances volitional receptivity.

This looping of the psychomoral act can be either efficacious or detrimental. Most germane to the psychomoralitic process is the loop that begins with the acceptance of the initial truth that the diminishment of the pseudo-self, the breaching of the ego defenses, and the abnegation of the ego is good in itself. This prevents the detrimental circularity of a counterfeit and temporary abnegating of the ego so that it can eventually be restored and increased. This counterfeit abnegation is a disciplined temporary acceptance of humiliation based on a pending gratification of the ego that will result from it. While this counterfeit abnegation tellingly is not a characteristic of symptomatic mental disorder but of high functionality, it is nonetheless the coping mechanism of delayed gratification and thus is not psychomoralitic.

7. THE PSYCHOMORAL REALM OF THE PASSIONS

THERE IS MUCH CONFUSION concerning the nature of essential mal-being, or more precisely its sometimes manifestation in ego-reactivity (and concomitant symptomatic mental disordering), because there is much confusion concerning the nature of the passions. William James equated passion with purely subjective experience, while Freud equated egoistic passion with the essence of the human person. Behaviorists equate all passion as emotional reactionary instrumental behavior, while humanists equate its unleashing with authenticity and actualization. More recently, many psychologists have given up trying to succinctly define the passions and rather say it is an amorphous conglomeration of all the above, and other components as well.

But because all of these theoretician's lack an adequate anthropological topography of the psychomoral realm, their definition of passion, like their conceptualization and treatment of symptomatic mental disordering, is doomed to err. Indeed, for the mental health profession, like all its mental disorders bottom line, the passions, or here more aptly emotions, are a physical phenomenon. This is because passions are always felt, and the mental health profession again falls into the fallacious reasoning of equating correlation with causation. Psychomoralitics does not deal with the emotions as understood by the mental health system, but rather treats the psychomoral realm of the passions.

Psychomoral well-being and the passions are intrinsically linked, thus the proper understanding of the passions is crucial to the remedying of ego-reactivity. In short, *ego-reactivity is ego passion binding of the psyche's reason and volition*. Thus a person under such an ego passion domination is to some extent irrational. Yet passions are in themselves a good. When properly marshaled, that is under the reign of the psyche's reason and volition, passions are absolutely essential for living a fully human life. As will be seen, the connecting of the passions and reason is done via love, which is uniquely both passionate and rational.

The Passions as Opposed to the Emotions

Psychomoralitics defines the emotions as a *physiological reaction* to the stimuli of impacting reality. Psychomoralitics defines the passions as a *psychomoral reaction* to the stimuli of impacting reality. But the human person as a hylomorphic being also reciprocally experiences the stimulation of the emotions as an impacting reality in the psychomoral realm and the stimulation of the passions as an impacting reality in the physiological realm. Thus impacting reality is a positive or negative stimulus that can circuit through the emotions of the body, and the passions of the ego and the psyche. Indeed, these very emotional and passionate responses to impacting reality become impacting realities themselves.

On the purely physical/physiological level the body experiences positive impacting reality upon bodily good as pleasure and negative impacting reality as pain. Bodily emotions that come from pleasure and pain emanate from the physiological realm as the instinct of physical self-preservation. Though quite akin to love based passion, the emotion of physiological instinct for self-preservation does not entail truly *human* love, which always entails the reason and volition of the psychomoral realm. However emotion does necessarily impact upon the psychomoral realm. Bodily pleasure and its concomitant physiological emotion will always entail actual, or the promise of, pleasure or at least its preservation, and thus bring in the psychomoral realm and its passions. Bodily pain and its concomitant physiological emotion will always entail actual or the promise of pain, and thus again bring in the psychomoral realm and its passions. Note that all positive and negative impacting reality can also stem merely from the imagination and memory, and this includes not only the higher psychomoral functioning, but even mere emotional and purely physiological body memory. This impacting reality of the imagination or memory can be either anticipatory, remembrances, or sympathetic.

On the psychomoral level there are two types of passions: that of the ego and that of the psyche. The ego experiences impacting reality upon its subjective good as either the stimuli of ego gratification and or ego abnegation. For the ego, positive impacting reality entails actual, or the promise of, ego gratification; and negative impacting reality will entail actual, or the promise of, ego abnegation. Thus the ego passions are evoked by the impacting reality of ego gratification or abnegation. The ego's passionate reaction here is both non-rational and rational, and may become irrational depending on whether or not it is ordered to the objective good of the psyche.

The psyche in the psychomoral realm experiences impacting reality upon the objective good as either the stimuli of gain of the objective good or the loss of the objective good. For the psyche, positive impacting reality entails actual, or promise of, gaining the objective good and negative impacting reality entails actual, or promise of, the loss of the objective good. Thus the passions of the psyche are evoked by the impacting reality of an objective gain and loss. Being keyed to an objective gain or loss, the passions of the psyche are in accord with reason.

The Chief Passion of Love

The passions have been traditionally categorized as love, desire and repugnance, delight and loss, hope and despair, daring and fear, and anger. This list can be expanded by delineating the plethora of "feeling" adjectives both positive and negative.[82] But no matter the delineation, the *chief passion* is

---

82 Affection, Anger, Angst, Anguish, Annoyance, Anxiety, Apathy, Arousal, Awe, Boredom Confidence, Contempt, Contentment, Courage, Curiosity, Depression, Desire, Despair, Disappointment, Disgust, Distrust, Dread, Ecstasy, Embarrassment, Envy, Euphoria,Excitement, Fear, Frustration, Gratitude, Grief, Guilt, Happiness ,Hatred, Hope, Horror, Hostility, Hurt, Hysteria, Indifference, Interest, Jealousy, Joy, Loathing, Loneliness, Love,

always love and the other passions are derivatives of this chief passion. The derivative *adjoining passions* come from either love of egoistic/subjective good or love of psychic/objective good. Love then is the chief passion, being the *sine qua non* of all the other passions.

Aquinas explains the passions as that which sets the person in motion toward an end desired, hence the etymology of e-*motion*. Aquinas further holds that the passions are set in motion by love as the beginning of the motion to the end loved. Thus love is the chief passion because love is the engine of willful action. Love is the passion essential to the fully human psychomoral act, and thus integral to the interplay between cognition and volition. When a person sees a truth cognitively he may choose to love it—desire or will it—as a good to share in, even in contradiction of other passions.

The chief passion of love is thus both a passion and a reasonable choice. *Love then is that which hinges the passions with rationality.* In this way, love can integrate and order physiologic emotion, and the egoistic and psychic passions. Love as a rational choice that gives precedence to the passions of the psyche is also the very engine of psychomoralitic change and general human maturation. Psychomoralitics, then, considers the passions not so much with an emphasis on concupiscence or irascibility, but

---

Lust, Outrage, Panic, Passion, Pity, Pleasure, Pride, Rage, Regret, Relief, Remorse, Sadness, Satisfaction, Schadenfreude, Self-confidence, Shame, Shock, Shyness, Sorrow, Suffering, Surprise, Trust, Wonder, Worry, Zeal, Zest.

rather on the object of the chief passion (that is, egoistic or psychic love) and the nature of the impacting reality.

The Summary Passions

For psychomoralitic purposes there are four passions that can be considered the characterizing summations of all the passions. These summary passions are directly resultant of the passionate choice to love either the subjective good of the ego or the objective good of the psyche that subsequently results in all the passions. Because of their direct proximity to the passion and choice of love, transcending the summary passions of the ego are key to reaching the point of the psychomoralitic act that is found in love.

The two summary ego passions are sadness and glee. Sadness sums up all the negative ego passions and glee sums up all the positive ego passions. Sadness, that is a self-pity, is the overall passion of the negative ego passions; whereas glee, that is a self-satisfaction, characterizes the positive ego passions. Anger, to some extent, will always be present with sadness, in that sadness or self-pity is an egoistic evaluation of reality as "unjust," that one "deserves better." So too anxiety is always present in egoistic passion, most abundantly in negative passion, but even in positive egoistic passion due to the covetousness of the ego.

The two summary psychic passions are *sorrow* and *joy*. Sorrow sums up all the negative psychic passions and joy sums up all the positive psychic passions. Sorrow, that is objective loss, is the overall passion of the negative psyche passions; whereas joy, that is objective gain, is characterized by the positive psychic passions. Whereas the positive and negative summary ego passions of sadness and glee can only intermix in the storm front of anxiety, the positive and negative summary psychic passions of sorrow and joy are integrally united in the calm of peace.

According to Aquinas,[83] the positive passion of *love* is inspired by the good loved, whereas the negative passion of *hate* is inspired by that which destroys the good loved. At the primary passion of love the psychomoralitic choice can be made to love the objective good of the psyche or the subjective good of the ego. This choice will subsequently determine whether one is dominated by egoistic sadness and glee or psychic sorrow and joy. In addition to being categorized as either psychic or egoistic, the other passions (here in their fundamental categories) are either positive or negative, and thus can be aligned accordingly

---

83 The positive passion of *desire* is inspired by a not yet attained good loved, whereas the negative passion of *repugnance* inspired by a destructive contrary of a good. The positive passion of *delight* is inspired by possessing the good loved, whereas the negative passion of *loss* is inspired by not possessing the good loved. The positive passion of *hope* is inspired by believing in future obtainment of the good loved, whereas the negative passion of *despair* is inspired by an unattainable good loved. The positive passion of *daring* is inspired by a difficult to obtain good loved, whereas the negative passion of *fear* is inspired by a danger to the good loved. Finally, the negative passion of *anger* is inspired by harm suffered by the good loved, harm perceived as unjust. All the passions above, save anger, are paired as positives and negatives. The negative passion of anger does not have a corollary positive passion because anger is a fighting against negative impacting reality, including all the other

under either the positive or negative summary passions. Note well, that due to the inherent subjectivity of the egoistic passions, it is characteristic for a positive passion to quickly transform into a negative passion and visa-versa.

Egoistic Passion

Egoistic passions emanate from their chief passion of love of an egoistic/subjective good. Egoistic passions find their beginnings in ego impacting reality that is either that of gratification or humiliation. Positive impacting reality to the ego is ego gratifying or aggrandizing. Negative impacting reality to the ego is ego humiliating[84] or abnegating. The positive ego passions come from gratifying impacting reality and the negative ego passions come from humiliating impacting reality.

---

negative passions. Anger's positive corollary is acquiescence or receptivity to these negative passions, which by definition is not a passionate reaction or response but rather an allowance of impacting reality, which includes the negative passions that are inspired by negative impacting reality. However, one could say that peace is the corollary negative passion to anger: negative in that it is a result of a non-exertion of the will. Note well that all negative passions will also necessarily entail the contrary of the chief passion of love which is hate, though hate itself and all negative passions are still based on love, because evil by definition means a privation of a good loved.

84 Humiliation need not be experienced as a typical shame or embarrassment, but is simply a description of the negative impacting reality that threatens and/or harms the ego.

The presence of gratification or humiliation is not ego-reactive passion, but is a precursor to it. At the point of egoistic impacting reality, a person may, due to egoistic love, choose a lower subjective good over and to the detriment of a higher, or intrinsically more lovable, objective good. At this point the passion of love and the ensuing passions may then bind the intellect to some extent, ranging from merely the impeded rationality of a coping's myopic selective reality to the irrationality of an extreme ego-reactivity's blindness to reality.

Psychomoralitics recognizes egoistic passions as involved etiologically in all ego-reactivity and sometimes in subsequent symptomology known as "mental disorder." Indeed, in much of the mental health field's criteria for so-called mental disorder, the overt presence of dominating and debilitating emotions (i.e., strictly physiological manifestations) is the prime criteria for diagnosis. This is especially apparent in the so-called "mood disorders," with *mood* itself synonymous with *emotional state*. But psychomoral egoistic passion is key to all ego-reactivity, not just those that may have similar symptomology of the so-called "mood disorders." For instance, psychomoral egoistic passions are key to symptomatic mental disordering when they manifest atypically as "inappropriate affect" or even when they are not manifested or markedly blunted[85] and repressed, for instance, in the symptomologies invalidly labeled as "Schizoid Personality" or "Post-Traumatic Stress Disorder." As with essential well-being

---

85 "Blunted affect" is indeed a passionate reaction. Feeling nothing or numb is still feeling the lack of something.

and mal-being, the correct understanding of the topography of the psychomoral realm provides a definition of passions that is succinct and hence readily applicable psychomoralitically.

Paradoxically, those who are in a habitual coping state may exhibit a certain calm and balance of the passions because of the efficacy of their coping mechanisms and thus non-manifestation of their egoistic passions. It is often the very fear of failing to keep the ego passions in check, and the ensuing vulnerability and *humiliation* entailed in their manifestation, that keeps a person in the coping state. But an absence of manifest egoistic passion is not synonymous with psychomoral well-being.[86] Indeed, maturation and the psychomoralitic process necessitates the letting down of coping mechanisms so that the ego itself is directly impacted by humiliating impacting reality. Unless a person is receptive to the impacting reality of humiliation, new or renewed avenues of approach will not be created and thus there will be no advance in psychomoral well-being.

In that it is necessary for a person to be receptive to the impacting reality of humiliation for maturation and psychomoralitic progress to take place, humiliation overall is not to be seen as undesirable if it is allowed to effect ego-abnegation. But, again, it is the very fear of not coping and possibly manifesting egoistic passion that often causes a person to remain in a coping state and thus only open to reality on a selective basis.

---

86 See Chapter 8: *Egoistic Coping.* p.139

Egoistic Anxiety

Anxiety is the ego specific manifestation of the passion of fear. Egoistic anxiety is necessarily concomitant to all ego-reactivity because by definition the ego is vulnerable and being threatened whenever the coping mechanisms are breached. Anxiety is concomitant even in overall ego-aggrandizement, even if only as a mild excitement to not miss an opportunity or lose out. But again, anxiety is most apparent in any resistance to a humiliating impacting reality that has breached the coping mechanisms.

Like all of the egoistic passions, anxiety can be present with or without ego-reactivity. But all ego-reactivity entails, initially and throughout, some element of anxiety. In a similar manner to the body's emotional fight or flight response when threatened with physical harm, the ego responds to the negative impacting reality of ego-abnegating humiliation with anxiety. In that the ego unchecked is its own reason for being, anything that threatens such an ego is anxiety producing indeed.

In the case of the negative impacting reality of humiliation and its concomitant passion of anxiety, the summary passion of sadness is a flight passion, whereas anger is a fight passion. The adjoining ego passions as well can be seen as either fight or flight reactions driven by anxiety. These ego anxiety driven fight or flight passions may bind the intellect and the will to the degree of the intensity of the humiliating impacting reality, the failure of coping mechanisms, and the resistance to ego abnegation. It is the anxiety driven fight or flight passions that constitute ego reactivity and its degree.

Psychic Passion

Psychic passions are based on the chief passion of the *love of an objective good*. This is a love of the objective good even when it is detrimental to both subjective physiologic and egoistic goods that are loved. This is where love of objective good takes place not because it is necessarily in a person's subjective best interest, much less because he feels good about it, but because it rationally *is*. This loving of objective reality entails the emotional impact of that reality, be it negative or positive, physiologic, egoistic, or psychic.

The *primary psychic passion of joy* refers to a positive passion that comes from psychic attainment or anticipation of the loved objective good. This psychic passion of joy is the fruit of loving and possessing an objective good. The *primary psychic passion of sorrow* refers to a negative passion that comes from the psychic loss of or threat to an objective good. This psychic passion of sorrow is a fruit of loving and not possessing an objective good.[87]

Joy and sorrow are always concomitant to each other. This is because joy and sorrow are the primary passions of loving the objective good, an objectivity that does not exclude any aspects of that good. Joy and sorrow coexist as a phenomenon that are never

---

87 Aristotle recognized that the passions of the soul are those passions "which are followed by joy or sorrow." *Nicomachean Ethics*, ii, 5.

completely isolated, enduring in peaceful coexistence in the depths of the human heart (i.e., the psyche). This is because joy and sorrow require an openness to reality that is not selective, and thus they do not bar one another. Both indeed accentuate each other: the greater openness to sorrow leads to a greater openness to joy and vice versa.

Because joy and sorrow admit of mutual coexistence, this may make them less singularly felt. So too, joy and sorrow are deep passions marked by peace and endurance and thus often experienced in a very subtle manner. This deep subtlety of psychic passion is especially evident in comparison to tumultuous or high-anxiety egoistic passions or urgent, but superficial, bodily emotions.

Joy is even more subtle than sorrow. Aquinas eludes to the more piercing manifestation of sorrow and the more subtle manifestation of joy:

> But here again we find a difference; because when this transmutation is for the worse, it has more of the nature of a passion, than when it is for the better: hence sorrow is more properly a passion than joy.[88]

Nonetheless, the deepest and truly human passion is found in the psychomoral realm, and ultimately in the psyche. Thus even physical stimuli, be it pleasure or pain has its most enduring and deepest effect psychologically. However though the passions

---

88 *Summa Theologica* , I-II Question 22.

of the psychomoral realm will be felt physically, the degree of physical manifestations does not necessarily correspond with the degree of impacting reality. Indeed, in the psyche realm, the joy especially can be extremely subtle, even ethereal, but thus more enduring and transcendent even among the more tumultuous vicissitudes of life.

When a person experiences physical pain it is accentuated by the moral anguish of anticipating its continuation, of not knowing when it will cease, or by foreseeing its future renewal. So too, the experiencing of pain and pleasure accentuates both: "Sweet is pleasure after pain."[89] This is true not only physically but psychomorally. It is only the proud that can be humiliated and the humiliated are eager for aggrandizement. But it is the experiencing of joy and sorrow, the openness to reality in its fullness, that accentuates both and indeed allows them to coexist in plummeting the depths and soaring the heights of the human experience.

Psychic Peace

As the ego passion of anxiety always is concomitant with the humiliation of impacting reality and the subsequent fight or flight passions, so too is the psyche passion of peace always concomitant with passions receptive to impacting reality. When one is no longer fighting or flying from reality one is, by definition, at peace with that reality. This peace, as well as the joy

---

89 John Dryden (Aug 19, 1631 – May 12, 1700).

and sorrow, becomes deeper and more abiding as a person matures in receiving-the-real, assenting-to-truth, and receiving-the-good; that is, as a person achieves essential well-being.

Ordering the Passions

When passions are properly marshaled under the reign of the psyche's reason and volition they are an essential impetus and ingredient for living a fully human life. The psyche must be given full reign to respond to the presence, plenitude, or promise of the objective good or as the absence, deficiency, or harm of the objective good. Only by means of the psyche and its dominance can a person be fully open to the good and the heights of positive passions. Only by means of the psyche and its dominance can a person find equanimity and peace in the presence of evil and in the depths of negative passions. Only by means of the psyche and its dominance can a person be peacefully open simultaneously to the joys and sorrows of life. Whether a person is advancing in psychomoral well-being and flourishing is determined by such an openness made possible by the dominance and choices of the psyche.

In both the physiological and psychomoral realm, that which set the person in motion is the reaction to impacting reality. When impacting reality is the negative of physical pain or the threat of harm to the body, the emotional reaction is that of fight or flight. While the body's emotional fight or flight mode may be difficult to quash completely, it may be diminished and overridden by either the ego and/or the psyche. Thus, for instance, a person may react in a non-rational or irrational manner to merely avoid humiliation or to acquire aggrandizement; or a person may endure pain in physical exercise by focusing on the rewards and the subsequent aggrandizement of the ego; or a person may via the psyche recognize the body for what it is and not allow the desire for physical-self preservation to unduly influence his rational choices; or a person may via the psyche recognize the ego for what it is and not allow the desire for ego preservation to unduly influence his rational choices.

Because of the human person's hylomorphic nature, physiology can quite often be the precipitant of ego-reactivity. But being a precipitant is not the same as being causative. For instance, a person may feel extremely depressed physiologically due to disease but needn't fall into psychomoral depressive self-pity (or its sometimes attendant mental depressive symptomology). This is because physiology is of a lower faculty than that of the psychomoral faculty, and being a lower faculty cannot mandate a specific response from the higher faculties.

However, the inverse is not true. A person's psychomoral state always has a physiological manifestation; the psychomoral realm of the rational *animal's* higher faculties necessarily influences the lower faculties. Thus ego reactivity that emanates from the psychomoral realm will always have a physiological manifestation. A person suffering psychomoral depressive self-pity, for instance, will always experience a degree of physiological depression. The fact that ego reactivity always manifests itself physiologically and that physiological disorder often precipitates ego reactivity is a major reason why the mental health field has deemed symptomatic mental disorder to have a biological basis. But this fallacious etiological conclusion is based on equating correlation with causation.

All of the passions can be used for the good and for an increase in maturation and psychomoral well-being. Thus a person could honestly assert, "I am happy that I feel humiliation,"when from a psyche perspective he realizes that such a feeling will abnegate his ego. A person can honestly say as well, "I am happy that I feel loss and sorrow,"when that loss and sorrow is the result of the psyche saying *yes* to reality. Happy indeed, if there be true happiness at all, is the person open to the fullness of reality.

A person can say *yes* as well to his very deficiency and inadequacy in the good as part and parcel of the good; for it is good in that his deficiency and inadequacy is true, even though it means accepting the ego abnegation and humiliation of one's radical contingency. This ability to so choose, to receive being, assent to truth, and love the good, inclusive of one's inadequacy and contingency while still fully desiring the absolute supreme good, is the essential drama of human existence. It is also the intensified condensed drama of the psychomoralitic process, the heart of which is the moment in which undiluted being, truth, and good are brought to the threshold of a therapant's innermost awareness.

8. EGOISTIC COPING

MUCH OF THE GARGANTUAN MENTAL HEALTH SYSTEM, and psychiatry and psychotherapy in particular, aims at helping a person to cope. A person is considered to be coping when he is functioning at a level deemed socially acceptable and possesses some semblance of contentment. This prescription for coping then entails a superficial externalism and takes a utilitarian approach that validates almost anything that helps a person "get by." But get by what? Relationships? One's past? The present? The future? Life itself?

Yes, coping is aimed at getting-by certain impacting realities of life itself by blunting those realities, most especially those that scale the heights of sublime joy, plummet the depths of profound sorrow, or engage in the dramatic battle between good and evil. But if life is merely something to be gotten-by, blunted, or endured, then the default position is despair. Thus the mental health system's goal of coping does ultimately end in despair, even though one may be anesthetized and deadened to that despair. But is it really a fully human life to just get by it? Or, as per psychomoralitics' aim, should intervention for essential human well-being facilitate a person's total immersion in existence and the human experience?

In the mental health field coping is specifically defined as "constantly changing cognitive and behavioral efforts to manage specific external and/or internal demands that are appraised as taxing or exceeding the resources of the person."[90] Coping is thus considered a successful conscious effort that protects the ego from that which taxes, exceeds, stresses, or conflicts with it. The mental health prescription of a reality blunting coping is diametrically opposed to that which is prescribed by psychomoralitics. Indeed, psychomoralitics prescribes the very allowance of that which taxes, exceeds, stresses, or conflicts with the ego, so as to abnegate that ego. This psychomoralitic prescription is the only possible way to achieve essential well-being and innermost peace, for the impacting reality of life *necessarily* entails "exceeding the resources of the person." It is the peaceful acceptance of the overwhelming dynamic of one's existential and specific condition that indicates a mature and psychomorally well person.

In the roller-coaster of life a person may cope by white-knuckling it, by keeping eyes myopically squinted and focused on a distraction so as to not see the dizzying heights; or a person may cope by anesthetization, keeping eyes shut tight and achieve some degree of somnolence and unawareness during the ride. But psychomoralitics aims at helping a person fully experience the impacting reality of the ride. Fully experiencing the ride of

---

90 Lazarus RS, Folkman S: Coping and adaptation. In *The Handbook of Behavioral Medicine*. Gentry WD, Ed. New York, Guilford, 1984, p. 282-325.

life entails facing directly and feeling acutely both the ups and downs of life: the steep, anxious and exhilarating ascents, the dizzying and exalting pinnacles, and the plummeting and transformational falls. And yes, even the inevitable mechanical failures and jumpings of the track.

By means of creating avenues of approach in lieu of coping mechanisms, psychomoralitics facilitates a person's openness to the full spectrum of reality. This full spectrum of reality entails both bottomless sorrow and unfathomable joy; passions that can be experienced integrally and even simultaneously. When a person is truly open to the full spectrum of reality, psychic sorrow melds with joy in the midst of an abiding peace for a full human flourishing. Psychomoralitics' goal is not to *cope with life* but to be *open to life*. Psychomoralitics is aimed at living life to its fullest; that is, at living in the full truth and goodness of one's existence. The fullness of life is indeed the "good life," for again the good is a synonym for truth, being, and the real; and the real is itself the essential touchstone of essential human well-being and human flourishing.

Two Types of Coping Mechanisms

The state of coping admits of two types of habitual mechanisms: the pliable and the rigid. With a pliable coping mechanism, though a person may rest in a certain selective openness to reality, he ultimately and habitually gives way to an insistent impacting reality regardless of its ego abnegating effects.

In pliable coping when the blunting of reality fails, a person may initially be in a state of ego reactivity, that is, egoistically and passionately reacting to reality and its ensuing humiliation; but he will nonetheless, when push comes to shove, eventually acquiesce to that reality. This giving-way to impacting reality entails subordination of the ego passions, abnegation of the ego, and the increasing of avenues of approach, openness to reality, maturation, and well-being. Thus a person with habituated pliable coping mechanisms is generally moving between coping and increased well-being with some temporary ego-reactivity in between. This process, which is the normal—but today increasingly uncommon—maturation process, is usually somewhat cyclical and gradual, as in two steps forward and one step back.

The rigid coping mechanisms occur in a habitual state that is steadfastly open only to selective realities and hardened against certain ego-abnegating realities. A person with habitual rigid coping mechanisms has developed psychomoral blinders. Like a horse with racing blinders, these psychomoral blinders keep a person on track by means of a limited awareness. When a person with rigid coping mechanisms begins to have these defenses breached he will most likely seek distractions and/or anesthetization. If these distractions and/or anesthetization fail, the person with breached rigid coping mechanisms is likely to become hyperselective in a frenzied attempt to cope and is poised to fall into manifest ego-reactivity. Thus a person with rigid coping mechanisms will characteristically move, if he moves at all, between ego-reactivity and increasing coping mechanisms.

Both a person with pliable coping and one with rigid coping admits reality incrementally, blunting that which is too painful or even merely inconvenient. But the person with pliable coping is characterized by an ultimate receptivity to impacting reality as it presents itself, even to the detriment of the ego; whereas the person with rigid hardened coping mechanisms is characterized by selectively allowing only that impacting reality that will in the long run preserve and increase the ego.[91]

Coping mechanisms whether pliable or rigid are ego generated. Although coping mechanisms are not as binding of the intellect and will as are reactive ego passions, they still have a reality blunting effect; and can even have a reality distorting effect. This is especially true of rigid coping mechanisms. It is from the point of ego impacting reality that the myriad of choices are made that either lead to an increase of avenues of approach, maturation, and well-being or an increase of coping mechanisms, ego passions, and mal-being. The choice to be receptive to impacting reality and increased avenues of approach leads to a character that is increasingly open to impacting reality and progressing in psychomoral maturation. Conversely, the choice to defend against impacting reality leads to a stunted character, psychomoral stagnation, regression, the risk of debilitating ego-

---

91 As such, in rigid coping even the admission of an elective humiliation can be such that it facilitates success and thus the ego's growth, as is the case with delayed gratification.

reactivity when that reality can no longer be blunted, and an increase of mal-being.

Coping is Superficial

The mental health field's go-to psychotherapeutic prescription for increasing coping is nothing other than the power of positive thinking (i.e., optimism). But optimism is not realism. Neither is pessimism realism; however studies do show that extreme pessimists are actually more in touch with reality than the mental health field's prototype optimist!   Indeed, optimism is an essential characteristic of coping, whereas extreme pessimism is an essential characteristic of an ego-reactivity marked by the summary ego passion of self-pity (sometimes accompanied by the symptomatic mental disordering known as clinical depression and almost always by its persistent low-grade cousin known as dysthymia).

Experimental research[92] has repeatedly produced the statistically significant conclusion that people with ego reactivity marked by the predominate ego passion of self-pity (also

92 Alloy and Abramson first introduced the notion of Depressive Realism in 1979, when one of their experiments gave rise to a significant result: people with moderate or sub-clinical depression turned out to present a more accurate perception of their cognitive control over reality than non-depressed participants. The phenomenon has been repeatedly confirmed in a series of successive experiments.   In a functional magnetic resonance imaging study of the brain, depressed patients were shown to be more accurate in their causal attributions of positive and negative social events than non-depressed participants who demonstrated a positive bias.

sometimes manifest in the symptomology labeled *major depression*), have a more accurate perception of reality than people without this passion (and ensuing symptomology). In other words, people with a manifest and habitual extreme self-pitying ego-reactivity have a more accurate perception of reality than people in the rigid coping state. The great quandary in these findings for the mental health profession is that persons with their designated mental disorder of depression have a greater awareness of reality than those without. It is the mental health profession's lack of a definition of *the real* as well as their essential correlation of functionality with "mental health" that disallows the integration of these dissonant findings into the profession's flawed conceptualization.[93] But the fact remains that these findings indicate that a person with symptomatic mental disordering, as a result of habitual and extreme self-pity, is in some ways more in touch with reality than those who are coping and considered "mentally healthy" by the mental health profession.

Unlike the falsely premised conceptualization of the mental health profession, psychomoralitics is easily able to integrate

---

(Seidel, E.M., Satterthwaite, T.D., Eickhoff, S.B., Schneider, F., Gur, R.C., Wolf, D.H., ... & Derntl, B. (2012). "Neural correlates of depressive realism —an fMRI study on causal attribution in depression." *Journal of Affective Disorders* 138: 268–376.

93 So too, it may be safely surmised that most functioning mental health clinicians are successful at coping themselves, and thus would be considered less in touch with reality—or at least better at denying it— than their therapants.

these paradoxical findings on optimism/reality blunting coping and pessimism/ego reactive self-pity into its conceptualization. For psychomoralitics makes the crucial distinction that though a person with ego reactivity may be experiencing impacting reality to a greater degree than a person who is coping (in that ego-reactivity is impacting reality's breaching of the coping mechanisms), such an ego reactive person is not *open* to that reality but rather is fighting or running from it. Conversely, a person who is coping is blunting impacting reality and thus not experiencing it to the same degree as one with manifest reactivity, but may still be more open to certain select realities, especially on the functional, ego-congruent, and superficial level. This selective openness to reality may allow some aspects of reality to pierce a coping person relatively deeply but, like a myopic set of blinders, a rigid coping necessarily compromises a waxing or full openness to reality that requires a diminishing or absent selectivity.

Delayed Ego Gratification

A person who is apt at and habituated in rigid coping will always have the ability to practice *delayed gratification,* which is the ultimate coping mechanism. Delayed gratification is the ability to select to be open to certain realities, even when those realities militate against his ego, for the future strengthening of the ego. In this a person is able to accept a certain abnegation of the ego and pseudo-self so as to become a better pseudo-self. Because the coping defense of delayed gratification entails an acceptance of a certain humiliation of the ego for the sake of preserving and ultimately aggrandizing the ego, it is also highly functional.[94] The coping mechanism of delayed gratification is found in the various forms of stoicism, from existentialism to cognitive behavioral therapies, and many forms of religiosity.

The ego coping mechanism of delayed gratification is characteristically unlike either the apathy or lethargy characteristic in common coping. Rather it may entail very proactive and aggressive activism. But it is still selective and restrictive of reality in the *single-minded* pursuit of a subjective good. Such coping is characterized by this single-mindedness, and a disproportionality or even obsession with selective goods to the exclusion and sacrifice of other—and at times even higher —goods. An example of such coping can be seen in overachievers such as the driven athlete, or the intensely studious graduate student, or the passionately ambitious politician.[95] Those well-practiced in delayed gratification may also appear very virtuous.[96]

Note well that people with manifest ego reactivity and/or symptomatic mental disordering are not good at coping, especially at the above supreme coping of delayed gratification, and thus a psychotherapeutic process that entails the ability to

---

94 Again,with functionality, along with feeling good, being a criterion for so-called "mental health."

95 Indeed, those most driven often are seeking to cope with a classic narcissistic wound of childhood.

96 See below, § *A Note on Stoical Existential Coping*, p.153 and Chapter 9: § *Beyond Virtue & Vice*. p.160

delay gratification is often futile. The goal of psychomoralitics, which facilitates its efficacy as well, is not to produce a coping person but a person beyond the coping stage and open to the fullness of reality.

Degrees of Coping

There has been an apparent contemporary shift in Western civilization toward increased rigid coping and habitual ego-reactivity and away from pliable coping and the ensuing gradual maturation. The shift to rigid coping as opposed to pliable coping has allowed for more people to fall into unresolved ego-reactivity and/or an increase in mal-being rather than to resolve ego-reactivity with ego-abnegation and increase in well-being. In short, when impacting reality hits and stresses the coping mechanisms and uncovers the ego passions, more people are tending to resist that impact rather than be receptive to it. Today's technology, with its myriad of anesthetizing distractions and offerings of soul-numbing medications, greatly facilitates and has even caused this trend.

In the absence of urgent impacting reality, coping is a common function that most people fall into at different periods in their lives; indeed, most people experience a shift to-and-fro coping throughout a single day. While this common coping is not proactive in the pursuit of reality, neither is it necessarily a form of rigid coping. At leastwise, a common coping marked by lackadaisicalness can be attributed to complacency and lethargy, and to the fact that most people are neither philosophers, poets, nor prophets. At best, maturing people when coping usually drag their feet in the direction of openness to and the embrace of reality.

Still the commonality of coping, be it pliable or rigid, does have very serious social consequences. For though this sort of coping is not marked by the commission of evil, it is marked by *omission*, and omission itself can be insidiously evil. It is coping that allows people, if and when they can, to turn away and ignore the suffering of others. Coping is what explains apathy. It explains, "How [apparently] good people can allow evil things to happen." It explains how apparently good people can even allow evil things to happen in their own name, as is common with crimes of the State.[97]

Naturally, if a person is in the process of opening up more and more to reality in a steady maturation, he is more unlikely to fall into the lethargy and apathy of common coping. Indeed, it is those proactively seeking and opening themselves up to reality—e.g., philosophers, poets, and prophets—that are the catalysts for the awakening of the rest of the populace. If a person is open to reality he will not consciously and consistently do, facilitate, or allow evil, which is in essence the rejection of reality; that is, the

---

97 Coping is the essence of not only apathy, but of cowardice as well, where a person does not do the right thing because it entails a threat to the ego's subjective good. Such ego generated cowardice can stem from the fear of calling attention to oneself by confronting the evil and thus being outside the power curve of the entity doing the evil (again, often the state), or even just the mere inconvenience entailed in a response.

rejection of the real, the true, and the good.[98] So too, such a person is proactive in his discernment of the cause and remedying of evil. Much as a physician must objectively encounter illness and its disease causing agent to remedy it, those proactively seeking to remedy moral evil must intentionally and objectively study and encounter it. It is the person, then, that goes beyond coping and is proactively open to objective reality that has the prudence and wisdom to discern what can and should be changed and what must be accepted.

Coping Toward Mal-Being

The coping mechanisms of selective embracing-of-reality are employed in protection of the ego's subjective good from the objective truth[99] of a threatening impacting reality. Again, the objective good is good because it is reality, not because a person likes it. The subjective selectivity of coping effectively bars those aspects of reality which are too unpleasant for the ego to bear. But the fullness of reality, the depths of human existence, will always be too much for the ego to bear, for ultimately it promises the annihilation of both the body and the ego.

Pliable coping can merely be a person's temporary foray into a carefree or even frivolous attitude that is the result of the

---

98 Evil is that which destroys a higher truth and good for the sake of a lower truth and good and hence is a denial or negation of the fullness of reality.

99 It is also an objective good, but because it may destroy a subjective lower good it is seen as evil.

presently impacting reality being relatively non-urgent and/or the proportionalizing of events. Such a frivolous or carefree attitude can even be based on being open to reality and thus placing things in their proper or proportionalized perspective. This differs from rigid coping, habitually maintains equilibrium, and thus restricts the dynamics of human teleology which is the maturation of an increased openness to reality.

As a habitual state, rigid coping comes from a person's solidified mechanisms against impacting reality. Rigid coping is the mental defensive phenomenon of selectively controlling the effects of impacting reality in a hardened and habitual manner. This ability to control impacting reality is determined by both the degree of impacting reality and the adequateness of coping mechanisms. A person is most likely to cope well when reality is not too adversely impacting. Thus those that have not experienced major failures in coping have usually not experienced brutalizing or out-of-season impacting reality where coping mechanisms[100] become inadequate. But even coping mechanisms that are adequate become inadequate in a proper ongoing maturation process.

Rigid coping is the selective denial of impacting reality, the blocking out of that which is an unacceptable threat or harm to the ego. Such unacceptable reality can range from personal

---

100 There are some, however, in the presence of such a deep traumatic reality (a.k.a., "narcissistic wound"), that cope with a functional ego reactive drive to succeed (a.k.a.., the "pathologically driven").

insults to universal cataclysms. By selectively vetting impacting reality a person impedes maturation by blunting that which pushes the perimeters of that maturation and embracing-of-reality. Paradoxically, denial of painful reality also impedes the enjoyment of joyful reality as well.   This is due to the superficiality that necessarily accompanies successful coping. This superficiality prevents a person from living the fully human life.

Again, because in the rigid coping state there is no overt passion binding the reason and will—exactly because there is no pushing of the perimeters of maturation—coping is commonly seen and promoted by the mental health system as the ideal psychomoral state. But at best, the state of rigid coping should be seen as a state where mal-being and ego reactivity are not manifestly present, and not seen as a state of well-being itself. Psychomoralitics conceives the coping state, both pliable and rigid, as the psychomoral or spiritual doldrums. It is the habitual rigid coping state that causes a person to be stunted in his embracing-of-reality and to stagnate upon the path of psychomoral maturation, openness to reality, and essential human well-being.

As coping increases there is a point where it transforms from an omissive act to a commissive one, where it becomes more of a rational choice to reject reality rather than just ignore it. This rational choice in its extremes becomes a malignant rejection of the real, the true, and the good. This malignant choice is an obduracy that is a conscious, fully rational turning away from Objective Being to the egoistic self, where one freely decides that they will serve their subjective contingent self. Ego-obduracy is the essence of evil[101] and rigid coping paves the way to it.

A Note on Stoical Existential Coping

Because of some commonality, it is important to emphasize the difference between the ego-abnegating nature of psychomoralitic existential awareness of reality and the ego-aggrandizing nature of ancient stoicism and its modern variant in existential psychology. Both psychomoralitics and existential stoicism correctly hold that a person cannot fight certain realities, specifically those deepest of realities, those ultimate concerns.[102] But the solution stoicism proffers is to not be bothered by these deepest and most impacting of realities. If these realities become too bothersome or insistent, that is if they no longer can be effectively ignored, then suicide is an option. Existential stoicism then is a high functioning ego coping mechanism that protects the ego from ultimate reality. Very strong, and apparently virtuous people, may function on this level. They are focused on what they can do; they are often high achievers.

---

101 While outside the scope of the present book, there is much to be addressed as per the psychomoral understanding of malignant coping and extreme mal-being.

102 For instance, secular existentialists identify the four Ultimate Concerns of human existence as death, freedom, isolation, and meaninglessness. Traditional Christian spirituality, which predated secular existentialism by some millennia, provided the philosophical placeholders for it in conceptualizing the four ultimate concerns as *death, judgment, heaven, and hell.*

But existential stoicism is a practiced selectivity of reality. It defends against the reality that a person cannot do anything about. But these ultimate realities are indeed ultimate, and openness to them is essential to entering into the full drama of human existence and to experiencing true human flourishing. Yes, these ultimate realities are the most devastating: the present reality of the irreversible past, its guilt, failure, and all the loss of the good now gone; and the present reality of the irresistible future, its suffering, death and all the loss of the good now had. Resigning to things one cannot change is rational, but not being bothered by these things, these ultimate realities, is not. To hold, "If I can't do something about it, it doesn't matter," is a the stoic's ideological coping defense of the ego. This defense is the arrogant, prideful refusal to be overwhelmed, even if it means taking one's life once one can no longer keep up the stoical pretense.

In the place of an openness to full reality, the existential stoic selects "engagements" that give transitory meaning to his life, thus allowing himself to be unburdened by the contemplation of the Ultimate Concerns. Modern existential psychology holds that wholehearted engagement in any of life's activities is the means to temporarily alleviate the inherent dysphoria (but not necessarily the anxiety) of existence. This subjective and select engagement, according to modern existential psychology, allows a person to pattern the meaningless and unassembled brute data of existence into a subjectively coherent, but artificial, whole. "Engagement does not logically refute the lethal questions raised by the galactic perspective, but it causes these questions not to matter."[103]

Such a stoical selection of only certain realities is nihilistic. For it is the nihilistic denial of the human desire for ultimate meaning and beatitude, of the very specific difference of the human being. This nihilism brutalizes and negates the very humanity of the person. "When it comes to meaninglessness, the effective therapist must help his clients to look away from the question."[104] But the question of meaning is the human question. Note that the stoical assertion that *the issue of meaninglessness is not a question leading to a a quest, but a given, stultifying fact,* not only denies the essence of humanity, but also absurdly frames the issue. For if there is no possibility of meaning there is no possibility of meaninglessness; that is. meaninglessness can have no meaning.

These engagements of stoicism and modern existential psychology are nothing more than coping distractions, or temporary defense mechanisms, against the most impacting of reality. In short, they are functional drugs of volition. Thus ancient stoicism and modern existential psychology swings from optimism (engagements) to indifferentism (a looking away or burying of the Ultimate Concerns) to pessimism (nihilism and the suicidal option); but it is manifestly not realism. For these prescribed engagements are but superficial distractions from

---

103 Yalom, I.D.; *Existential Psychotherapy*; Basic Books, New York (1980); p. 482.

104 *Ibid.*; p.483

ultimate reality; the inherent subjectivity therein is by definition not objectivity; the indifferentism but an ignoring of a devastating uncontrollable impacting reality; and the nihilism but the ultimate brutalization of the human spirit's defining desire for truth, good, and beatitude.

Indeed, secular existentialism's identified four Ultimate Concerns of death, freedom, isolation, and meaninglessness are posited so that one can be *ultimately unconcerned* about the call of human existence. Death becomes an oppressive monster of brutalizing tyrannical fear and hopelessness. Freedom becomes but a slavery to an irresistible impulse to satiate one's basest passions and anesthetize any discomfort. Isolation becomes set in the stone of a closed-off egoistic self-orientation. And with meaninglessness, one becomes inhumane and scornful of his responsibilities as a rational, volitional being. In so far as there is a denial or lessening of the possibility of receiving-the-real, assenting-to-truth, and choosing-the-good, there is a denial or lessening of the human vocation; that is, of man's specific difference and any possibility of essential well-being.

9. Essential Well-Being

Psychomoral maturation and the increase of essential well-being are synonymous. Human maturation and the increase of essential well-being entails actualizing the psychomoral realm's potentiality for receiving-the-real, assenting-to-truth, and choosing-the-good. The actualization of this potential is greatly influenced by a person's character, that is, his specific manner of ego defenses, predominate passionality, and avenues of approach. A person's character begins to be formed in early childhood with the gradual onset of reason and becomes firmly established as a person ages and becomes habituated in the specific manner and ways in which he defends the ego, is passionate, and is receptive to reality.

Impacting Reality

Character is made up of various combinations and proportions of coping mechanisms, ego and psychic passions, and avenues of approach, all of which are reactions or responses[105] to impacting reality. Impacting reality can come to a person in many ways—from physical trauma to existential angst. This trauma and angst can have its origins in the remembrance of

---

105 The ego *reacts* and the psyche *responds* to impacting reality.

the past or in anticipation of the future, but it is always a new or renewed present threat to the ego. For present impacting reality includes not only new or deeper impacting reality but the accomplished reality of the past and the potential reality of the future. All impacting reality then—past, present, and future—is to some extent present impacting reality.

The past is always present in that it has happened and thus can never be undone, even if it is felt less acutely over time. Ego-reactivity is often a result of a subconscious attempt to escape or change a past trauma. But so too, those in a coping state without overt manifestations of ego-reactivity will at some time—even if it only be in the throes of death[106]—be brought to an awareness of the traumatically impacting reality that exists beyond their superficial and artificial awareness.

In addition to past impacting reality, future impacting reality is as well always present. Future impacting reality is present in potentiality. As with past realities, future potential realities in essence are always present and, though their specifics may change, they will become actualized in a person's life sooner or later. This presence of the *potential inevitable future* is especially threatening in regards to future vicissitudes, sickness, and death.

---

106 However, today's *status quo* medicine in conjunction with status quo psychology seeks to anesthetize a person even at this most dramatic time of human existence. Thus "death with dignity," is but death without awareness. But death is not dignified, rather death is the ultimate humiliation, but thus an ultimate, that is final, opportunity for maturation in physical existence.

Characterological Formation

Whether a person is on the path of increasing maturation and well-being, stagnating, or on the path of increasing mal-being, depends on the dynamics between characterological formation and the degree and specificity of impacting reality. This is a dynamics of continual psychomoral acts made—that is, the defending against, or receptivity to, impacting reality—that results in a person's character. In a progression of time and repetition, a mere thought will lead to a single act; an act repeated will form a disposition; and an enduring disposition will become a habit. It is this process and dynamics that forms the character, which is the set conglomeration of habits.[107] Here the psychomoral process, in its experiential (receiving-the-real), cognitive (assenting-to-truth), and volitional (choosing-the-good) aspects, plays out.

Whether a person is habitually open to reality, habitually closed-off, or a combination of both is determined by the summation of his psychomoral acts. The uniqueness of a person's character, building on natural aptitudes and deficiencies, is formed by the specificity of the psychomoral acts made. This uniqueness of character is comprised of specific manners of coping, specific dominant ego and psychic passions, specific

---

107 "Sow a thought reap an act; sow an act reap a habit; sow a habit reap a character; sow a character reap a destiny." (Anon.)

avenues of approach; and the relative strength and interactive combination of these.

Beyond Virtue & Vice

Ordinary, or acquired, virtues are *apparently* rightly ordered. However ordinary virtues can be rightly ordered on a lesser level, but wrongly ordered on a deeper level. An act ultimately ordered toward the aggrandizement of the pride may be superficially ordered, but it is ultimately disordered or, at the very least, imperfect. In so far as ordinary virtues are not built upon the primary psychomoralitic virtue of receptivity,[108] they are only superficial virtues. If ordinary virtues are ultimately means to defend or aggrandize the ego then they are false virtues. While true and habitually chosen avenues of approach may be conceptualized as ordinary virtues, and habitually chosen ego defenses may be conceptualized as ordinary vices, that which *appears* or is considered as "virtuous" or "vicious" may not be, respectively, actual avenues or ego defenses.[109] Thus apparent ordinary virtues are more aptly viewed as acquired disciplines rather than virtues when applying the psychomoralitic standard.

---

108 See Chapter 11: § *The Psychomoralitic Virtue of Receptivity.* p.200

109 An apparently humble man may simply be retreating or flying from that which is humiliating. An apparently arrogant man may be accepting the humiliation of confronting or fighting an evil. The issue is not whether the pride and self-love are to some extent present, but as to whether they are the key factor. Will the obsequious man no longer retreat but stand up to evil no matter the humiliation? Will the fighting man continue to fight no matter the humiliation?

A person in the coping state may be considered virtuous because he is not being challenged by, or is not open to, an urgent and intense impacting reality. Or a person may be considered virtuous due to the disciplined implementation of temporary ego-abnegation through an ego motivated delayed gratification, which is surely disciplined but not necessarily ego-abnegating. Conversely a person may be considered vicious because in heeding a higher good he harms a lower good, but that higher good is not recognized by others—due to viciousness, superficiality, or unawareness—but the lower good is.

Again, those that are not coping, including those with severe ego-reactivity, are not necessarily more advanced in mal-being than those that are coping. Rather the severely ego-reactive have been pierced with an impacting reality that has made a choice imperative and actualized their potential mal-being that lies dormant in a coping state. Nor are those more advanced in well-being necessarily without manifestations of ego-reactivity, which due to their lessening concern for humiliation is not well-hidden and will wax and wane as they advance upon the path of ego-abnegation.

Indeed, both those in a solid coping state and those well advanced in mal-being may rarely, if ever, manifest overt ego-reactivity; that is, they appear virtuous. Those on the advanced end of mal-being are truly opposed to reality in their commissive choices of rebellion, whereas those on the coping end, the proverbial lukewarm, in their omissive choices, ignore reality. Thus due to these paradoxes of ego-reactivity and the possible superficiality in evaluating virtuousness and viciousness, the categories of virtue and vice by themselves are not adequate to measure psychomoral maturation and essential well-being.

In that the character is comprised of coping mechanisms, ego and psychic passions, and avenues of approach, it is either tending toward or being open to reality, or tending away from or being closed to reality, or the various combinations thereof. A closed character will have a rigid manner of coping, dominant but functionally ordered ego passions, and limited avenues of approach. An open character will have a pliable manner of coping, few dominant, even if sometimes manifest, psychic passions, and many and increasing avenues of approach. The unique combinations and relation of the manner of coping, the passions, and the avenues, as well as the specificity of the impacting realities that are either being resisted or received, determines the true character of a person; that is, whether a person's character is receptive, pliable, and open *versus* resistant, selective, and complacent. There is also the malformed character that has inadequate coping mechanisms that give way to the domination of unbridled ego passions.

Characterological formation, then, entails an individual uniqueness in the manner in which a person is receptive and resistant to reality and to specific realities. To begin with, each person has experiences that are unique, beginning in utero and continuing through early development. So too, each person's physiology and neurology is unique in aptitude and inaptitude and thus is unique in its sensitivity[110] to certain forms of reality. Thus people vary as to which particular realities are harder or easier to accept. The combination and specificity of, and relation between existing and imminently potential new avenues of approach and that of ego defenses and imminently potential new ego defenses, is the unique sum of character. This combination of specificity and the relation of the ego defenses and avenues of approach also determines how ego-reactivity or abnegation unfolds in an individual, and thus is of the essence in efficacious diagnosis and remedial treatment.

The characterological building blocks of the psychomoral act are the assent or non-assent to truth and the choosing or not choosing of that truth as the good. Characterological formation is constantly taking place because impacting reality is constantly present. There are also times of a very intense increasing of impacting reality. However, once characterological habituation is established, it is strongly determinative of a person's response or reaction to impacting reality. If ego defenses have been established that do not yield to impacting reality but rather deny, fly from, or fight that reality, then intentional efforts (e.g., through the practice of psychomoralitics) to replace these ego defenses with avenues of approach are required.

---

110 Sensitivity to certain impacting reality varies among individuals because in the process of knowing the human person receives reality through the senses, which vary in accord with physiology, and ultimately through the neurological organicity, which varies as well.

But note well, that just as the categories of common or acquired virtue and vice do not suffice for psychomoralitic measurement, neither does their summation as a virtuous or vicious character suffice. Those considered to have a virtuous character on a certain level are not necessarily correspondingly advanced toward essential well-being, and those who could be considered to have a vicious character on a certain level are not necessarily correspondingly advanced toward mal-being. Indeed, here paradox often reigns supreme, where the apparently most virtuous may be the most advanced upon mal-being and the apparently most vicious may well be most advanced upon well-being.

Early Characterological Formation

The development and increase of pliable coping mechanisms is best facilitated by an overall and gradual waxing openness to impacting reality resulting in the curtailment of egocentricity. If however, egocentric rigid coping mechanisms have been habitually formed, they tend to harden in their selective and limited openness to reality. The gradual and habitual formation of either pliable or rigid coping mechanisms, the underlying ego passions' degree of domination, and etiological subordination of, or insubordination of, the ego to the psyche, takes place foundationally in childhood.

Infants are not, strictly speaking, "egocentric" because they are unable to differentiate and choose between their subjective good and objective good, which is due to their lack of reasoning ability. Infants are, however, totally "selfish" in that their awareness is limited to their subjective bodily and emotional experience. Indeed, the in utero child experiences little distinction between himself and his mother and carries this on postpartum. As an infant matures they become more aware of the differentiation between themselves and others and the environment. Developmentally the ego comes into being with the increase of reasoning ability and the ability to discern and choose.

The development of the ego markedly begins, give or take some months, in the anecdotal "terrible twos". The terrible twos (or often threes) is a traumatic time for the child. The child begins to realize that he is not the center of the universe because he begins to differentiate himself from that universe, from his mother, his father and siblings, and from objects. This becomes somewhat traumatic when the child begins to realize that reality, parents, siblings, and things do not always conform to his desires, wants, and needs. Indeed, now the child begins to experience that often he needs to conform to reality. Thus begins psychomoral maturation and the struggle between a nascent ego and reality.

The psychomoral struggle between a nascent ego and reality within the child can be epitomized in the trauma of toilet training. In this developmental milestone a child is asked to substantially modify a very intimate and constant activity. Indeed, all of a sudden something the child does is no longer acceptable, it is even deemed unpleasant (e.g., foul or filthy). At this time, the child may also be confronted with a new infant sibling that jarringly takes his place as the focal point of the family. Reality itself, being now at times obviously contrary to the child's subjective desires and good, begins to take on hostile, even frightening, attributes. Thus the common occurrence of nightmares or night terrors.

This advent of reasoning ability, and subsequently the ego, is a subtle and gradual process that reaches a certain threshold of discerning ability at around the age of seven, where a child is able to clearly discern the difference of right and wrong according to an overt and superficial letter of the law. However reasoning ability is still not fully developed even unto adulthood, with the organic myelination of the frontal lobe continuing to develop through adolescence and early adulthood. But reasoning ability should find its final capping in older age where, though cognitive skills may decline, wisdom and a deep understanding of the spirit of the law will shine forth if a person has continued through life to mature and grow in openness to reality.[111]

Inherited Dispositional Defect

The development of the ego, that is of pride and self-love and the ensuing mechanisms, is part and parcel of human development, but whether or not a person is disposed so that the ego eventually gives way to the greater reality of objective truth

---

111 Because impacting reality increases as one ages, its greater denial must also increase if one is attempting to cope. Thus rigid coping or mal-being will also increase through time. Thus old age and cognitive decline brings with it either wisdom or dementia.

and good over its own subjective good, is the issue of proper childhood development. Developmentally, as per the human intellect being *tabula rasa*, a person begins to know and reflect upon himself only by coming into contact with an external reality. As per irrefutable empirical evidence, all men are born with concupiscence, a darkened intellect, and a weakened will. This inherited dispositional defect can become exacerbated by external reality, creating a self-awareness that is inordinately focused on self.

This exacerbation of man's inherited dispositional defect can occur during childhood development for a variety of, and even paradoxical, reasons. On one hand, a child may never receive enough authentic love and affirmation from his parents and may feel this deprivation acutely. As a consequence the child must subconsciously continue to egocentrically fixate on self; that is, subconsciously increase his love of self because if he does not love himself no one else will. Such a child lacks the parental love that allows him to turn from his infantile egocentrism. On the other hand, a child may be overly indulged and spoiled by his parents. Such parents are ultimately acting out of their own self-love and seeking their own gratification, the end sought being the child's reciprocal affections. As a result the child's fixation on himself is reinforced. In either cases of neglect or over-indulgence, the parent's ego generated self-love is dominant and thus only solidifies the child's own self-love and egocentricity. Here a child may obey merely to protect or aggrandize his ego and/or he may rebel for the same reason.

For a child to begin the maturation process properly requires the presence of authentic parental love. Parental love is the prototypical *sacrificial* love. Sacrificial love derives from the psyche rather than the ego. A child will only have the courage to let go of his ego's subjective good, that is, to turn from his subjective self love, if he experiences a parental love that is greater than his ego generated self love. Because sacrificial parental love is of the objective truth and psyche, and may be willed even to the detriment of the parent's own ego, it necessarily transcends egocentric self-love. It is this true parental sacrificial love instilled in the child that is the essence of proper childhood formation.

The maturation process begins in childhood and exactly requires that the child begin to let go of his egocentricity and open himself up to the greater reality. Again, a child that does not adequately experience a greater parental love will not have the courage to undergo a budding ego's abnegation or to open himself up to a greater reality. Such children when they become adults may well have to deal with unbridled ego-reactivity and mal-being. Indeed, if the terrible twos are not properly dealt with the terrible twenty-twos, etc., will loom in the future.

Out-of-Season Impacting Reality

Impacting reality can be at times so intense that any and all coping mechanisms are breached and the ego passions are manifested. Throughout life a person is called to be open to greater and greater impacting reality by choosing to forgo these mechanisms and passions in a receptive abnegation of the ego and thus mature and grow in essential well-being. But there are levels of impacting reality that are age or developmentally appropriate; that is, that are more readily accepted and facilitate maturation and an increase of essential well-being.

However, out-of-season impacting reality that is brutalizing also occurs. Even toilet-training if done too early or forcefully can become mildly traumatic. But events with a impacting reality much more brutalizing can occur as well. Such out-of-season impacting reality can be amoral, such as the death of a parent or sibling or one's own illness or disability; or it can be immoral, such as occurs when a child is the victim of a vicious act.[112] Without proper intervention (that is, informal or formal psychomoralitic intervention) out-of-season impacting reality is too much for a child at his developmental stage to either cope with or grow from, and may well manifest in a present or future ego-reactive and a markedly mal-adaptive turn from reality.

A child of five is not expected to be a man of sorrows, but nor should a man of fifty be unable to enter into sorrow. Tragically, it is often the young child so overwhelmingly challenged that becomes the adult so stifled in maturation. But it is here that psychomoralitics proffers the remedy. Psychomoralitics can transform a past brutalizing impacting reality from a festering, even if buried, debilitation into an accelerating catalyst for a

---

112 Though even here a child can be helped to process the reality in a psychomoralitic way, if his caretakers themselves do so.

superlative openness to reality, and thus essential well-being and maturation.

The *Sine Qua Non* of Maturation and Essential Well-Being

Impacting reality that breaches the coping mechanisms may either lead to dominant ego-reactive passions and/or ensconced mal-being; or, if impacting reality is receptively allowed to breach the coping mechanisms, transcend the ego passions, and thus abnegate the ego, it may lead to a person's increased openness to reality both in breadth and depth. This is the intended maturation process of the human person and the waxing of essential well-being. This volitional openness allows the depths of the psyche to be penetrated. In such an increased openness, the psychomoral pain of reality not only remains but increases, both in the humiliation of the ego and the sorrow of the psyche. An increased receptivity to psychomoral pain is the *sine qua non* of both maturation and essential well-being. As a person matures and increases in well-being, psychomoral pain is felt more acutely because impacting reality is allowed to abnegate the ego and penetrate the psyche. But because the psychomoral pain of humiliation to the ego is not fought, the dynamics is not an anxiety ridden back and forth between reality and the ego's coping mechanisms and passions, but a relatively peaceful acquiescence to that painful humiliation and the abnegation of the ego.

When the pain of impacting reality is allowed to penetrate to the psyche it is experienced as the passion of sorrow. Thus when a person is open to impacting reality, in addition to experiencing a greater humiliation, he also experiences a sorrowful pain. Yet this pain is a beneficial pain. In addition to the choice not to fight impacting reality with the ego defenses, which entails an ensuing peace, the locus of the pain itself shifts to the depths of the psyche and thus transcends the ego and its passions, making the humiliation tolerable because it is not final.[113] Thus the pain experienced in an increasing openness to reality is an acute, clean, and piercing pain that does not have the confusing, obtuse accompaniment of dominant ego passions, and the abnegation of the ego itself lessens in the acuity. The pain that strictly pertains to objective reality brings with it a peace, for reality is not fought and, as will be seen, opens a person up to positive passion as well, which in the psyche is experienced as joy.

The Path of Essential Well-Being

The person with pliable coping mechanisms and subordinated ego passions, when mandated to acquiesce to humiliation by an insistent reality, truth, and good, eventually does so, no matter the damage done to the ego. Thus in the end a person on the path of increasing maturation and well-being does not selectively limit his openness to reality in accord with his limiting coping mechanisms and underlying ego passions. Rather,

---

113 See Chapter 11: § *Stages to the Psychomoralitic Moment.* p.197

such a person allows impacting reality to cause a psychomoralitic state of flux. In this psychomoralitic process and state of flux—be it formal or informal—a person chooses to allow limiting coping mechanisms to be eradicated, the ego passions to be transcended, and the ego to be abnegated by increased avenues of approach. The psychomoralitic act then, allows impacting reality to abnegate the ego and unencumber the psyche.

Note well that the development of a mature character permeated by avenues of approach does not mean that such a person is unthreatened by impacting reality, or even without initial resistance to impacting reality. Rather, it is a question of eventually choosing to say *yes* to that reality even though it means diminishment of the ego. Thus, those actually in the process of ego-abnegation may go only "kicking n' screaming," but go they do, whereas those ensconced in rigid coping mechanisms or in the depths of mal-being may be exteriorly placid, but interiorly defensive of the ego.

A person that has pliable coping mechanisms, subordinated ego passions, and the habitual pattern of a psyche dominated ego will still have defensive coping selectivity, but this selectivity is finally secondary to psychic receptivity; he does have ego passion, but these ego passions are not finally dominant; and he does have egoistic subjective interest but this subjectivity is secondary to the objective good. Again, for most people, such a *yes* to impacting reality is often issued in receptive surrender only when their backs are to the wall, that is, when their egos are confronted with an unrelenting and insistent humiliation of impacting reality. But such maturing people, unlike those with rigid coping, no matter the ego-reactivity that may manifest itself in the process, will at the end of the day acquiesce to the humiliation and the abnegation of the ego and advance upon the path of psychomoral maturity and essential well-being.

10. Ego-Reactivity

Neither those in the state of ego-reactivity, nor those in the state of ego-abnegation are fully coping with reality. A person with ego-reactivity is manifestly not coping because he is not effective at *selectively* blocking or blunting the impacting reality that is unacceptable to the ego, but rather by definition is traumatically overwhelmed by it. So too, a person receptively undergoing ego-abnegation is not coping because he is not blocking out the impacting reality that is unacceptable to the ego, but rather by definition is open to the humiliating reality proffered.

The breaching of the coping mechanisms allows the direct encountering of the ego and evokes its passions, and this makes possible either an increase or decrease of essential well-being. Thus, those in ego-reactivity and those in ego-abnegation have something in common: *both are experiencing the breaching of the coping mechanisms*. At the point of where a negative impacting reality breaches the coping mechanisms there are two opposite responses possible for either an increase or decrease of psychomoral well-being.

In the presence of an irresistible negative impacting reality, ego-reactivity begins with the continued but futile struggle of the ego to cope in a hyperselective or frenzied manner. Here the hyperselective and ineffectual coping mechanisms are joined by the ego's passions which begin to overtly manifest and exert themselves. Conversely a psychic reception of irresistible or intentionally chosen impacting reality abnegates the ego and increases avenues of approach that pierce to the inner depths of the psyche.

Thus a person in either the state of ego-reactivity or the state of ego-abnegation may be experiencing a greater degree of impacting reality than a person in the state of coping. But whereas those in the state of ego-abnegation are peacefully receptive to this reality, those in the state of ego-reactivity are desperately resistant to it. It is the hyperselective, frenzied and futile attempts to cope with or resist impacting reality and the subsequent emergence of ego passions that are the essential dynamics of ego-reactivity.

Ego-Reactive Passionality

Psychomoral ego-reactivity entails the ego passions. Such passionality is characterized by the presence of concomitant anxiety, the summary ego passions of sadness/anger or glee, and the adjoining ego passions. The degree to which these ego passions are manifest and dominate is the degree of ego-reactivity. Note well that mal-being may be present in the absence of ego-reactive symptomology, and is not intrinsically tied to quantifiable dysfunctionality.

While the positive ego passions of gratification can lead to mal-being and may occasionally dominate in an irrational ego-reactivity, it is the negative ego passions of fight or flight that are the cause of enduring ego-reactivity. This is because it is the avoidance of pain, and here specifically humiliation, that drives a person to habitual ego-reactive behavior. While the positive ego passions may lead to ego-reactive acts, they are usually counterbalanced by the fact that these acts in the long run cause more pain than pleasure. This results in the person who is ego-reactive to the positive impacting reality, inevitably falling back into a coping state where there is cessation of avoidable pain, which itself is gratifying, and some semblance of a balance stuck between gratification and pain.

However, with the negative summary and adjoining ego passions driven by the concomitant ego passion of anxiety, the dynamics of humiliating impacting reality and reactive ego passions are urgent and often unrelenting. It is the avoiding or the escaping of pain, not the pursuit or experiencing of pleasure, that usually drives a person to do things that in themselves are remarkably vicious, harmful, and/or highly irrational.

Ego-Reactive Anxiety & Stress

With the onslaught of negative impacting reality, a person non-receptive to it will initially experience the ego passion of anxiety. Anxiety is thus the precursor and continual common denominator of all ego passionate reactivity. Though the ego anxiety here is experienced physiologically or emotionally, as is all human passion by definition, it is not essentially a bodily reaction to physical threats but to psychomoral threats to the ego. But even physical threats, in their accentuation of bodily vulnerability and weakness, find their final impact in a threat to the ego.

Psychomoral ego anxiety is a result of the impacting reality of gratification or humiliation, but it is most overwhelmingly experienced as a result of humiliation. Here the mere threat of humiliation is itself an experienced humiliation because the very *possibility* of humiliation indicates the vulnerability of the ego. If coping mechanisms are not able to deal with this humiliation, then their breaching will begin to take place, compounding the threat to the ego because one realizes the humiliation of not being able to "handle" the situation.

So too, the emergence of anxiety and other unwanted secondary ego passions are humiliating in and of themselves and in their uncontrollable manifestation, thus feeding upon themselves. At this point, an unreceptive, resistant person tries to "hold it together," that is, tries to maintain the pseudo-self and its rigid coping mechanisms in protection of the ego. This is an exhausting psychomoral endeavor that, again, only exacerbates the anxiety. Anxiety is also accompanied by *stress*. Stress is the pushing back against the threat signaled by anxiety. Generally speaking, stress is the result of two opposing forces. Just as a ship's hull is stressed by the waters that surround it, the ego is stressed by the humiliating reality that surrounds it. The obvious key then to the alleviation of stress is an acquiescence to the threat that causes one to be ego anxious.

Psychomoralitic Point of Flux

The beginning of all psychomoralitic change is found in the disruption of the pseudo-self by an impacting reality's breaching of the coping mechanisms and the ensuing direct impact upon the ego with its passionate reaction. At this point of initial decompensation[114] the integrity of a person's composite pseudo-self begins to be compromised and his psychomoral equilibrium disrupted. This occurs with both pliable and rigid coping mechanisms.

This initial stage of decompensation is the psychomoralitic point of flux. If this decompensation is ineffectually resisted it can result in ego-reactivity that is new, relapsing, temporary, or habitual, and/or the increasing of rigid coping mechanisms. But this initial stage of decompensation can also result in the transforming of rigid coping mechanisms into pliable ones, the diminishment of pliable coping mechanisms, and/or the supplanting of ego defenses with avenues of approach. Note well, that it is the actual resistance to decompensation that brings on and exacerbates ego-reactivity. In other words, it is the very "trying to hold *it* together," with *it* being the pseudo-self, that is the problem. Whereas instead, as psychomoralitics advances and

---

114 Decompensation: The functional deterioration of a previously working structure or system.

facilitates, it is the peaceful "letting *it* fall to pieces" that is the key to an increase of well-being.

When a rigid coping mechanism is initially breached due to its inadequacy, it usually becomes accentuated in an attempt to defend against the impacting reality. Such accentuated coping mechanisms attempt to dampen down the ego passions which are strongly present. When this accentuated coping is unsuccessful and the impacting reality unrelenting, then coping becomes hyperselective, ego passions are irrepressibly manifest, and the beginnings of an increasing ego-reactivity takes place.

If a person reacts to impacting reality in a resistant manner, then openness to reality becomes further constricted. Because impacting reality is being fought and an attempt to maintain the pseudo-self is being made, there is no peace but rather anxiety, stress, and ego fight or flight passions. Here either coping mechanisms are efficaciously increased or ego-reactivity is increasingly manifest. Whether a person copes or falls into increased ego-reactivity is dependent on the degree of impacting reality and adequateness of coping mechanisms. If the ego-reactivity does increase it can be temporary or chronic. If only temporary, it can be resolved as either a psychomoralitic lessening of coping mechanisms, the ensuing abnegation of ego and reduction of its passions, and an increased openness to reality. Conversely, temporarily increased ego-reactivity can resolve in a reinstatement and solidification of coping mechanisms, and to a further aggrandizement of the ego itself and the subsequent increase of its passions.

Definitions, Degrees, & Durations of Ego-Reactivity

The psychomoral state of a person waxes and wanes in accord with various factors that increase a person's sensitivity to impacting reality. Physiological sensitivity can be heightened by, for instance, hormonal changes, illness, aging, or even diet. This physiological sensitivity necessarily has psychomoral ramifications in that man is a hylomorphic being. So too, the intensity and specific nature of the impacting reality varies greatly, which may be especially painful to a particular person with his specific coping mechanisms and prominent ego passions. Thus a person will feel the impact of reality to a greater degree at certain times.

The progression of ego-reactivity from non-manifest to mild to moderate to severe is as follows:

➢ Non-Manifest Ego-Reactivity informs *rigid coping* and, to a lesser extent, *pliable coping*, as a stable and functional selective openness to reality. Here coping mechanisms allow ego-reactivity to remain indirect and relatively hidden.

➢ Mild Ego-Reactivity is when the ego passions cause coping mechanisms to be hyperselective as per a disproportional and imprudent reasoning and volition. Here coping mechanisms struggle to maintain equilibrium of the pseudo-self and become anxiously hyperselective and manifest the traits of the underlying ego passions.

- ➢ Moderate Ego-Reactivity is when the ego passions cause *coping* mechanisms to be hyperselective in an illogical or unreasonable manner. Here coping mechanisms begin to fail and decompensation of pseudo-self begins with anxiety and other ego passion manifestations.

- ➢ Severe Ego-Reactivity is when overt and unbridled ego passionality admits of only highly distorted, erratic, and discombobulated coping mechanisms. Here the coping mechanisms are ineffectual and ego passions bind the intellect and the will, which ensues in ego-reactivity that is dominant.

Any of the above degrees of ego-reactivity admit of various durations: from temporary, to dispositional, to habitual. Ego-reactivity's degree of severity coupled with its duration determines its consistency. A person with habitual non-manifest ego-reactivity will display the most consistency, whereas a person with habitual severe ego-reactivity will be the least consistent.

Ego-Reactivity Nosology

Ego-Reactivity may or may not correspond symptomatically with the superficial symptom based nosology[115] of the mental health profession. This is because psychomoralitics does not ascribe to the mental health profession's bedrock criteria of functionality as determinative of "mental health." Indeed, in

---

115 Nosology: Classification of disease.

psychomoralitics it is not a question of mere, and often arbitrary, correct mentation and behavior but essential well-being.[116]

While the DSM has defining criteria for diagnosing specific mental disorders, it does not have a succinct definition for mental disorder itself. This is because the DSM's nosology is based on symptomology not etiology. This symptomatical classification only allows the DSM to recognize so-called mental disorder but not define it; that is, to state that a certain manifestation is a mental disorder but not to say what is mental disorder.

In contrast, psychomoralitic nosology is not based on symptomology but on etiology. This is made possible by an understanding of the psychomoral topography of the human person. Thus, utilizing this psychomoral topography defines ego-reactivity as the reaction of the ego to impacting reality with passions that interact with and subsequently bind the intellect and will. Whereas this definition provides the etiological definition of ego-reactivity, the specificity of the ego-passions, including their combinations and degrees of intensity, provides the symptomatic definition.

It is in accord with the symptomatic manifestation of the ego passions that specific ego-reactivity can be classified or described.

---

116 With functionality as its criteria the mental health system promotes the utilitarian view of the human person, a view that justifies a quantitative valuation of a human person's worth and leads to a myriad of crimes against humanity, with not a few being committed by that mental health system itself.

But because of the recognition and primacy of psychomoralitics' etiological or causative nosology, symptomology is secondary, and even non-essential, in the psychomoralitic diagnosis and intervention. In psychomoralitics it suffices to classify ego-reactivity according to the dominant passions and the coping mechanisms they inform. The whole plethora of secondary ego passions[117] will be either characterized as positive with a desire for or enjoyment of the subjective good, or as negative with an abhorrence of or opposition to, the subjective bad, with a further characterization as fight or flight in regards to the negative passions.

However, it is only the avoidance of the subjective bad, the humiliation and abnegation of the ego, that leads to severe ego-reactivity. This is because the pleasure factor becomes both satiated and diminishing in returns. Indeed, heeding the pleasure factor in the extreme can cause a net gain of pain. It is therefore self-regulating. Pain however can be unrelenting and increasing. Indeed, fleeing from or fighting ego-abnegating reality may well lead to an increased ego-reactivity, which in turn may lead to an increase of ego-abnegating reality—the humiliation of overt and uncontrolled ego-reactivity.

There are only two categories in which these ego passions fall: either fight or flight ego defenses. Most flight ego-reactivity would be those that stem from self-pity, which has a sometime symptomology of so-called "depression." Most fight ego-reactivity would be those that stem from anger, which has a

---

117 See Chapter 7: § *Egoistic Passion.* p.128

sometime symptomology of "mania." But note well, self or egoistic pity and egoistic anger are but two sides of the same coin of pride and self-love, and thus may be, and usually is, present as an admixture of both. Further cataloging or description of ego-reactivity is here omitted so as to emphasize both the simplicity of the psychomoralitic nosology as well as the secondary importance of that descriptive symptomology.

A Note on Ego Obduracy & Mal-Being

Ego-Obduracy increases with mal-being. Ego-obduracy is commissive, whereas coping is merely omissive. Ego-obduracy is rational whereas ego-reactivity is passionate. In sins of volition/passion the locus is the act and the ego, via its passions, bind the intellect and the will. In sins of reason/malice the locus is the choice and the ego is chosen by the intellect and the will and the ego passions are ordered accordingly. The more ego-obdurant and ensconced in mal-being a person is the less he is merely ego-reactive. This is because mal-being entails the use of reason and freewill in obdurately choosing the good of the subjective ego over the good of the objective real. Whereas ego-reactivity is the result of the ego, ego-obdurancy is the actual rebellious choice that creates the black hole of the ego, the mal-being of pride and self-love. This ego-obdurant choice that is the very creation of the ego, is a prideful turning away from *being in its supreme form* (viz., *Supreme Being*) for love of self. It is therefore both the primordial and culminating choice of human existence, but as a choice it can also resolve as an intellectual assent to the Supremely Real, the Supremely True, and the Supremely Good, which necessarily also entails an acceptance of one's contingent, non-supreme creaturehood.

Ego-Obdurancy goes beyond ego-reactivity and specifically entails the chief passion of egoistic love and prideful fixation on self. The degree that egoistic love and prideful fixation on self dominates indicates the degree of mal-being. The presence or absence of the summary or secondary ego passions are not indicative of the degree[118] of mal-being since the chief ego passion of love is capable of volitionally subduing these passions; indeed such a capability is characteristic of a person of severe mal-being.[119]

---

118 It is here advanced that those who have engaged in mass-murder sprees, young adults especially, are not necessarily cold-blooded murderers, but rather due to previous heavy use of psychotropic medication, they have become desensitized to impacting reality. The prevalent profile of these mass murderers is that of a young man who was as a child excruciatingly sensitive and fearful (because they were quite unable to cope with their humiliations), but after psychotropic use, and for that matter psychotherapy, became an insensitive and hate filled killer.

119 An absolute egotistic love of self may require demonic facilitation, as an absolute self-abnegating love of reality requires divine facilitation. The devil himself is completely sane.

11. The Psychomoralitic Prescription

PSYCHOMORALITICS FACILITATES SUFFERING-WELL the pain of both past, present, and future, so as to increase openness to reality, maturation, and essential well-being. Indeed, psychomoral trauma is the essential curative element of the psychomoralitic process. It is this essential curative psychomoral trauma that the mental health profession seeks to mitigate or avoid. Because humanistic sciences of well-being are more than just theory, but ordered to *in vivo* application, the diametrically antithetical orientations of psychomoralitics and the mental health profession result in the most fundamental and dramatic of contrasts.

The mental health profession, and specifically its psychotherapies, aims to assuage the ego and prevent its injury and abnegation. Conversely, psychomoralitics facilitates a therapant's suffering-well the abnegation of the ego. The mental health profession holds the ego to be the default essence of the person. For psychomoralitics, the soul is the essence of the person and the ego is at best an imperfection, and at worst a damnation. As such, much of what the mental health profession views as a human bad, psychomoralitics views as a human good, and visa-versa.

Psychomoralitics is strikingly opposed to the mental health profession in its prescription of the very psychomoral pain that the mental health profession seeks to anesthetize. A secondary consequence of this diametrical opposition is psychomoralitics' serendipitous alleviation of the very symptomology targeted by mental health treatment, as well as psychomoralitics' ability to reverse the subsequent harm caused by that treatment. Psychomoralitics is indeed the antidotal alternative to the failed and harmful mental health professions.

The Psychomoralitic Paradox

The goal of psychomoralitics is to facilitate in the therapant the breaching of ego defenses by impacting reality so as to abnegate the ego via the creation of avenues of approach unto the psyche. This psychomoralitic process increases openness to reality and essential well-being. In entering into the psychomoralitic process, a therapant must learn to suffer-well the impacting reality of psychomoral pain both past, present, and future.

Deep suffering, even if done well, is necessarily a traumatic experience. But in the psychomoralitic process, trauma is not brought to the therapant, rather trauma is brought to light so as to no longer be buried alive and left festering within the dark recesses of the psychomoral realm. Psychomoralitics brings the therapant into the light of reality so that he is no longer afraid, stunted, and debilitated by an insidious lurking psychomoral trauma.

A therapant's receptively feeling bad in the psychomoral realm is the *sine qua non* of psychomoralitic progress. This is because the psychomoralitic process takes a therapant down deep; and deep down, beyond the realm of superficial coping,[120] every person feels bad; indeed here every person feels wretched. Deep down, the human person feels wretched because of his vulnerable incarnational status; because of his basic contingent existential condition; because of the specific negative impacting reality of his life; because of his personal failings and weaknesses; and because of the presence of universal sorrows and evils. The mature person of essential well-being is in touch with and suffers-well these deep negative feelings and is receptive to the impacting reality that causes it.

But because the mature person of advanced essential well-being is widely and deeply receptive to impacting reality, he also experiences a myriad of positive feelings and is able to holistically integrate them with the negative feelings. So too, being receptive to impacting reality means a person is not resisting it, thus a fruit of this receptivity is an abiding peace. Conversely, the person whose coping mechanisms are overwhelmed and exhibits ego-reactivity feels bad but does not suffer it well, nor is he receptive to the impacting reality that causes these feelings. This ego defensive resistance to the impacting reality that causes humiliating psychomoral pain also results in a curtailment of a person's experiencing of positive impacting reality, and especially precludes fully experiencing the passions of the psyche. Finally,

---

120 See Chapter 8: *Egoistic Coping.* p.139

resistance or fighting of psychomoralitic impacting reality necessarily excludes peace.

It is feeling bad that usually causes a person to seek the help of the mental health profession, be it in the form of psychotropics or psychotherapy. Thus a person seeks psychotropics or psychotherapy to alleviate the psychomoral pain. But, paradoxically, it is the psychomoral pain that is the very antidote to the soul-deep etiology of targeted mental health symptomology. It is the proper acceptance of psychomoral pain that is the very catalyst and harbinger of innermost peace of mind, maturation, and essential well-being. No wishful thinking, nor psychotherapy, nor medication, can change reality and its painful psychomoral aspects. But psychomoralitics prescribes the transformation of these unavoidable painful aspects of existence from disabling to enabling, utilizing them as avenues to fully and harmoniously experience sorrow and joy and as catalysts for human flourishing.

Those very negative feelings caused by traumatic impacting reality, negative feelings a person has expended untold amounts of psychomoral energy trying to escape, are now, in psychomoralitics, sought as a catalyst for psychomoral tranquility. Those very feelings that have at best lurked in a debilitating manner within the deep recesses of the soul, and at worst caused habitual ego-reactivity, will now, in psychomoralitics, be a catalyst for peace and increased essential well-being. Those very feelings that were seen only as curses will now, in psychomoralitics, be seen as, and turned into, blessings.

But note well, that if the traumatic impacting reality was caused by either another person's immoral or vicious acts or one's own immoral or vicious acts, the act itself is not held as good. Rather, it is the psychomoral pain that emanates from the immoral or vicious act that is held to be good. For in the acceptance of the humiliation to the ego and sorrow to the psyche that resulted from a vicious act, the therapant is able to stop that act from festering in the psychomoral realm and free himself from its infection.

More so, the full acceptance of the humiliation and sorrow will not only undo the psychomoral harm of the act, but will bring about human flourishing, and bring it about to a superlative degree! Here, indeed, is a curse turned into a blessing. In proper maturation a person undergoes a natural, gradual, and non-clinical psychomoral progression. The end results of such a developmental maturation are similar to those of a therapant successfully undergoing intensive psychomoralitics. However in psychomoralitics, not only is the process condensed to the point of abruptness, but the results too are superlative to the point of miraculous.

Trauma: Past, Present, and Future

Throughout life a person is called to respond to greater and greater impacting reality, even if that reality impacted years ago. The pain of the past is always present, for it can never be undone.

The pain of the past may not be consciously present, indeed may even be suppressed and buried, but the defenses that so do the suppressing are themselves evidence of the past's ever-abiding presence. The suppression of past experiences is especially prevalent when the impacting reality was traumatic and/or out-of-season.[121] Again, certain levels of impacting reality are age or developmentally appropriate. When impacting reality is too brutalizing, defenses are built that can lead to rigid coping or habitual ego-reactivity. Psychomoralitics turns such an out-of-season impacting reality from a festering, even if deeply buried, debilitation into a psychomoral catalyst that accelerates openness to reality and thus full human maturation and essential well-being.

Psychomoralitics is specifically necessitated by the disruption of a gradual process of maturation. The disruption of gradual maturation is due to an out-of-season trauma that can be either from a happenstance occurrence or from an intentional commission of an overwhelming negative impacting reality. It can also be from the mere absence of a positive impacting reality, such as, and especially, the lack of paternal love.

In lieu of a proper and gradual maturation, psychomoralitics facilitates a more abrupt, and even jarring, maturation or openness to reality. But the abruptness and jarring impact is derived solely from that which is already present, again even if deeply buried, within the therapant: the psychomoral existence of a traumatic and resisted impacting reality. With this greater

---

121 See Chapter 9: *Essential Well-Being.* p.157

abruptness of psychomoralitic maturation that is necessitated by the presence of persistent ego-reactivity also comes a unique opportunity to enter into an accelerated maturation that does not even entail the blunting defenses of permeable coping mechanisms found in the normal or gradual maturation process.

Indeed, psychomoralitics utilizes the very presence of trauma that has been an impediment to maturation and essential well-being as a catalyst for these. In doing so, the coping mechanisms and passions of the ego are transcended completely in an accelerated maturing or psychomoralitic manner. This is the key to psychomoralitics' efficacy and the mental health professions' inefficacy. For those who suffer persistent ego-reactivity, and the symptomology of so-called mental disorder, have manifestly not been able to successfully order their egos unto reality. Thus the mental health professions' attempt to develop adequate coping mechanisms for an already disordered pseudo-self, has superficial results at best. Psychomoralitics not only recognizes that such efforts are ultimately futile but that the very lack of adequate coping places the therapant in a propitious position for positive psychomoralitic metamorphosis.

In psychomoralitics, unlike mental health psychotherapy, it is not the memory of actual or imagined occurrences that is of utmost importance. Rather it is the passional experience and impact that is associated with that memory that is of utmost importance. There is no clinical doubt that recovered memories can be notoriously inaccurate. But the recognition of this does not discount the psychomoral experience of a person who has these memories. These memories and the extent of their traumatic nature accurately convey the psychomoral trauma a person has had, and has. A person with recovered memories first feels the trauma passionately, then labels[122] these passions with what is perceived to be the source. Whether these memories are indeed memories, or imaginations, or a mixture of both, is psychomoralitically non-essential. What is essential is the psychomoral trauma that exists. Thus even the accuracy of the memories of events are not essential for psychomoralitic treatment, and their validation should not become a stumbling block.

Another reason not to focus on the actual historic events is that those historic events deemed objectively equivalent to each other do not necessarily subjectively affect different persons equivalently. So too, the recounting and focusing on the actual past events can re-traumatize in a way that reinforces ego defenses, and this is counterproductive psychomoralitically. Finally, because the facts of the traumatic event cannot be undone, it is not the facts that should be focused on psychomoralitically, but rather the passionate, that is felt rather than labeled, psychomoral trauma that is present.

---

122 This very labeling or designation of the source of psychomoral pain is itself a means to control, and hence cope with and rid oneself of that pain.

Forgiveness vs. Forgetfulness

In regards to past trauma, mental health professionals and others often prescribe the coping mechanism of forgiveness. Here a person will unilaterally "forgive" those that have hurt him so as to get past or be done with that hurt. Such supposed unilateral forgiveness also allows a person to feel virtuous as well. But unilateral forgiveness is not possible, rather it is an intentional and defensive forgetfulness that only buries the hurtful offense. For true forgiveness has as its prerequisite the victim's full acceptance of the psychomoral pain of an offense against him.

In fact, true forgiveness is by definition a bi-lateral process that occurs when the hurt is shared in a receptive manner by both the victim and the perpetrator. In forgiveness, the perpetrator is humbled and sorrowful; that is, the perpetrator is receptive to the humiliation and sorrow of his committed offense, rather than fighting it. So too, in forgiveness the victim is forgiving; that is, the victim is himself receptive of the pain of the offense against him and not reacting egoistically or revengefully against it. It is thus when both perpetrator and victim *share* the psychomoral pain of the offense that true forgiveness occurs.

Without a penitent perpetrator, the best a victim can do unilaterally is to be receptive to the pain caused to him and therefore not allow it to fester in the realm of the ego. This receptivity places the victim in the position of proffering forgiveness if and when the perpetrator is also receptive to the pain he has caused the victim. Again, it is the receptivity to the pain itself, the humiliation and sorrow, that allows a victim to be free of the festering hurt and debilitating defenses that can occur in reaction to an evil done unto him. Pretending one is over an offense, by unilaterally saying, "All is forgiven," is but a coping mechanism that allows that offense to fester, even if buried deep.

Objective & Introspective Appraisal of Psychomoral Pain

The psychomoral pain of egoistic abnegation is truly the cutting edge of psychomoralitics. But in order for a therapant to undergo this abnegation willingly it is necessary for him to see the pain it entails as a good. Understanding and accepting that ego-abnegating pain and subsequent psychic sorrow as good is the essential paradoxical truth of psychomoralitics. To apply this personally, a therapant must go beyond a subjective egoistic appraisal of psychomoral pain and achieve an objective psychic appraisal of it.

From an objective psychic appraisal of the abnegating ego pain, a therapant is able to choose to dominate the ego's subjective appraisal of it's pain as bad. In doing so, a therapant is able to become receptive as opposed to defensive in response to that egoistic pain. Here it is important to note that the ego's experiencing of the abnegating pain as bad is correct in regards to the ego itself, for the pain will hurt, humiliate, and abnegate the ego. But it is from the objective vantage point of the psyche that a therapant evaluates and chooses the pain of abnegating humiliation as good because it is indeed bad for the ego.

To be able to so see and choose the pain of egoistic humiliation as an ultimate good requires that a therapant not only assent cognitively to psychomoralitic principles, but also acquire them as an *objective introspective awareness.* This objective introspective awareness is a therapant's consciousness of the underlying dynamics taking place within his own psychomoral realm. This awareness takes place within the three stages of the psychomoral act: existential, cognitive, and volitional.

Stages to the Psychomoralitic Moment

In the first existential stage of *receiving-the-real,* the therapant *experiences* the dynamics of his psychomoral realm. To do this, the therapant must objectively experience the psychomoral impact of reality that occurs *before* the ego reacts passionately. This is to experience the primary impact of painful humiliation, which is the ego's existential experience of negative impacting reality. Again note that this humiliation[123] is not itself a passion but rather a catalyst for the passions. However, the ego's defensive passionate reaction is often instantaneous to that of the primary pain of humiliation, and thus the humiliation becomes subjectively indistinguishable from the ego's defensive passionate reaction. There is the need then for a therapant to distinguish experientially the primary impact of humiliation from the subsequent ego passions, which is the psychomoralitic task in the existential stage.

---

123 However shame as a response to humiliation is a passion.

Once the impact of reality is experienced in the existential stage, the therapant in the cognitive stage of assenting-to-truth is guided to reflect upon and understand the experience of raw ego impact in accord with the topography of the psychomoral realm. Here the therapant sees that it is indeed the entity of the ego that is being impacted. This leads to experiencing and knowing that *the ego is part of oneself, but not an essential part*. Identifying the ego with one's essential self is the basis of ego-reactivity and rigid coping. If the ego is equated with oneself, then any serious threat to it is a mortal threat and will cause anxiety, panic, and ego-reactivity. Here one believes that if the ego dies he will die. This is false. The truth to be realized in this cognitive stage is that though the ego is now part of oneself, it is not an essential part. Indeed, if the ego dies one will live! The final conclusion in the cognitive stage is the simple assenting to the truth of the real (as per the preceding existential state) as the good (as per the subsequent volitional stage).

The Psychomoralitic Act

Thus the psychomoralitic process requires the stepping back from the ego's passions—especially anger and self-pity—and then no longer opposing the humiliating reality that causes the stress and anxiety. Once a therapant realizes deeply that the abnegating impact upon his ego is good the actual psychomoralitic abnegation itself can be entered into in the volitional stage by a choosing of the humiliation of the ego as a good. It is this point of choosing to acquiesce to the humiliating experience of the initial negative impacting reality, that is the very psychomoralitic act. If the humiliation of the impacting reality is acquiesced to receptively and suffered-well, then the ego passions weaken, anxiety and stress recede, and peace ensues.

The psychomoralitic act is simplicity itself, for in essence it entails the most basic reasoning and choosing. After all the precursory deliberation, the psychomoralitic act is finally binary; that is a 0 or 1, *yes* or *no*, rational-volitional process. This is a *yes* to suffer-well ego-abnegating objective reality and a *no* to the egoistic subjective good. The psychomoralitic act is simple as well because suffering-well is a simple receptive act, a mere choice to not exert the will against reality, versus a more vigorous and complex exertion of the will.

So the psychomoralitic act all comes down to issuing a *yes* to reality; again, a *yes* that, to some extent, includes a psychomoralitic *no* to the egoistic self. This abnegation of the ego requires that its defenses be breached by avenues of approach that allow impacting reality to pierce through the ego to the psyche. The increase or maturation of psychomoral well-being is exactly the lessening of the ego distortions and obscurations of impacting reality—from the past, present, or future—and the broadening or creating of avenues of approach to the psyche. These avenues of approach, especially in psychomoralitic intervention, are created in lieu of debilitating ego defenses.

The Psychomoralitic Virtue of Receptivity

The essential psychomoralitic virtue is that of receptivity. The psychomoralitic virtue of receptivity is not exactly an acquired virtue as in an *exertion* of the will, nor an infused virtue[124] that is a supernatural gift, but rather a virtue in between that occurs when a person *chooses not to exert his will* and implement defenses against an infusing impacting reality. Again,[125] psychomoralitics defines virtue and applies the terms *avenues* and *defenses* more strictly and succinctly than that which is commonly regarded as *virtue* or *vice,* and the psychomoralitic continuum does not necessarily correlate with a continuum of apparent virtue and vice.

Whereas common acquired virtue may be a mere ordering of the ego in congruence with the psyche, the psychomoralitic virtue of receptivity is by definition not congruent with the ego. Psychomoralitic receptivity is the infusing of impacting reality and thus can be considered as active natural powers perfected,[126]

---

124 The infused virtues infuse themselves, whereas the psychomoralitic virtue of receptivity allows for the infusing of reality.

125 See Chapter 9: § *Beyond Virtue & Vice.* p.160

126 *Summa Theologica, Treatise on Virtue,* Question 55: *The essence of the virtue.*

"'*Virtus* denominates the perfection of a power or faculty with respect to its act. Some powers (*active natural powers*) are determined to their acts by their nature and so are called '*virtutes*' in themselves. But others (*rational powers*) are not determined to one act, and so they are subject to habits which provide them with perfecting "second natures," as we say. These are called virtues. See *ad* 2: "The act of a virtue is nothing other than the

specifically the power of receiving-the-real, where the infusing of the real takes place unimpeded, and facilitated by assenting-to-truth as a simple *yes* to the truth of the real, and choosing-the-good as a choice not to exert the will against the real and true.

Whereas common acquired virtue is habitual, the psychomoralitic virtue of receptivity never becomes habitual, for it entails not an exertion of the will, but the choice not to exert the will. The psychomoralitic virtue of receptivity could be said to be the non-habituation of exertions of the will against impacting reality. Thus the psychomoralitic virtue of receptivity is always fully free and thus fully human. So too, whereas common acquired virtue can be congruent, and even based, on pride, the psychomoralitic virtue of receptivity is based on humiliation. In the ego-abnegation of the psychomoralitic process one cannot become habituated to the humiliation nor any ensuing sorrow, because it always hurts, that is, it always goes contrary to nature, be it the nature of the ego or the psyche.

Psychomoralitic receptivity—like the infused virtues—in its very lack of habituation does not have the durability of ordinary acquired and habituated virtues, but can be lost in the very psychomoralitic moment. But so too, psychomoralitic receptivity need not ever be stressed to the breaking point as are all acquired

---

good use of free choice." That is, every virtue as a determined power is ordered toward a good use of free choice. The fact is, of course, that because the rational soul has various powers, there will be many habits (virtues) so ordered." (55,1)

virtues. Psychomoralitic receptivity, in its very lack of habituation, is spontaneous and never need not suffice, rather it can always take place in the moment by the choice not to exert the will.

This receptive nature of the psychomoralitic *yes* means a therapant needn't be strong or disciplined or enabled with acquired virtue[127] to begin the process. Indeed, the therapant's weakness, haplessness, and wretchedness become the very stuff of the psychomoralitic process. In short, that which has previously been a negative curse now becomes a positive blessing. This is done by saying *yes* to the painful humiliation and sorrow that accompanies one's failures, to one's very failure in the past to issue such a *yes*. This is, in short, saying *yes* to feeling bad about oneself. For it is receptivity to the pain that is the very remedy to ego-reactivity and the very catalyst for growth in maturation and essential well-being. In short, psychomoralitics utilizes the same catalysts that repercuss in ego-reactivity as the catalysts that repercuss in the remedial process and produce human flourishing.

Psychomoralitic Love

The psychomoralitic act is that which abnegates the ego, and ego-abnegation takes courage. It is love that gives a person the courage to be psychomoralitically receptive, to endure humiliation and sorrow. This psychomoralitic love is choosing the good of

---

127 Indeed the ability to delay gratification can often hamper the deep psychotherapeutic process. See Chapter 8: *Egoistic Coping.* p.139

reality over the subjective and lower good of the ego. Yes, the psychomoralitic virtue of receptivity is an act of love. The psychomoralitic virtue of receptivity is a natural infused virtue that is fueled by, if not a supernatural charity, at least the love of reality.

If "charity covers a multitude of sins,"[128] then the psychomoralitic act motivated by love of the objective good transforms a multitude of vices. It is psychic love that imbues a person with the courage necessary to allow a multitude of vices and defenses to be transcended so as to undergo a psychomoralitic ego reducing abnegation. Here again the psychomoralitic virtue of receptivity transcends ordinary virtue and vice. Indeed, the psychomoralitic act can utilize a vice as a catalyst for the good when one is receptive to the humiliation and sorrow that providentially accompanies that vice. Does the vicious but sorrowful person all of a sudden acquire ordinary virtue? No, the vicious but sorrowful person is all of a sudden humbled and contrite as he practices receptive virtue.

To choose to enter into the fullness of reality and human existence requires courage, and the only way a person can have the courage to live is to love reality, to love the good, the true, the real, being, and Supreme Being. Love infuses one with courage. Love transcends the sorrows of this life and so enables one to enter fully into those sorrows. It is only this transcendent love of reality that allows one to suffer fully. This love does not produce a detachment that causes one to hurt less, but rather a

---

128 1 Peter 4:8.

transcendence that allows one to suffer-well. The love that allows a person to embrace transcendent suffering also enables a person to rejoice freely and flourish as a human person.

But life is not all suffering and sorrow. Indeed, there is pleasure and joy in abundance. But once more, it is the presence of the pleasure and joy that accentuates the suffering and sorrow, and visa-versa. This is why some fear too much pleasure and too much joy. The impacting reality one typically fights is usually negative, but sometimes it is positive, for gain makes one more painfully aware of and susceptible to loss, and sometimes a person does not deem it "better to have loved and lost, than to never have loved at all."[129]

But it is only those who courageously choose to enter into the fullness of reality, including the pain of humiliation and suffering, who can experience the fullness of pleasure and joy as well. But such pleasure and joy is not that of an opiate that only seeks to kill the pain and suffering, for the pain is accepted throughout the pleasure and joy. It is this very ability to integrate suffering and sorrow with pleasure and joy that is the hallmark of those who choose to courageously love the fullness of reality and enter into as well, the fullness of human flourishing.

Psychomoralitic Peace

Psychomoralitics does not pretend to have the power to take away suffering, be that suffering of the body, ego, or psyche, but

129 Alfred Tennyson (6 August 1809 – 6 October 1892),

it does offer to teach a therapant how to suffer-well in light of the pain and thus experience peace, maturation, and growth in essential well-being. Indeed, it is the very attempt to avoid unavoidable and other certain sufferings either through distractions, anesthetizations, and/or ramped up hyperselective coping that is the tragic error of the mental health profession.

But since most are driven to enter into psychotherapy, or more fortuitously psychomoralitics, because of the psychomoral pain, a therapant may well ask, "What is the point of entering into treatment if the pain is not alleviated?" The answer is the acquiring of psychomoral peace. Innermost peace is the fruit of psychomoralitics. In so far as a therapant learns to be fully aware of and say *yes* to the piecing of impacting reality, no matter the abnegation of the ego and sorrow of the psyche it entails, he will be filled with peace. In the issuance of this psychomoralitic *yes*, a therapant gains both peace, joy, and abiding well-being amidst the humiliation and sorrow. The art of psychomoralitics is all ordered towards facilitating this *yes*.

The efficacy of the psychomoralitic *yes* is due not only to the simple binary reasoning involved, but also to this *yes* being totally receptive in nature. In saying *yes* to impacting reality a person is choosing *not* to fight it. Thus the psychomoralitic choice, though an act of the will, entails a choice to *not exert* the will against impacting reality. The psychomoralitic *yes* is thus a choice to acquiesce. In this choice not to fight, a peace necessarily ensues. This peace, while not banishing the painful humiliation of the ego or deeper sorrow of the psyche, nonetheless banishes the anxiety and passions of ego-reactivity. This peace is the hallmark of suffering-well and the promised fruit of the psychomoralitic process. So too, in addition to an acquisition of peace, a reservoir of energy is obtained in no longer having to fight the humiliation and sorrow with an exhausting exertion of the force-field of ego defenses.

In addition to the peace of receptivity, psychomoralitic peace also ensues when a therapant goes from fixating on *the particular* to an awareness of *the universal*. As psychomoralitics proceeds cyclically—from existential receptivity to cognitive assent to volitional embrace—a deeper personal piercing and empathy occurs in conjunction with a wider universal awareness. When one successfully says *yes to* the particular painful incidents of one's life, he necessarily opens himself up to a greater reality via increased avenues of approach. In this greater openness his own particulars are commingled with the pain of others and of existence itself, and thus he no longer obsesses about those particulars which are now proportionalized. So in addition to the peace and energy that ensues with no longer fighting the humiliation and sorrow, the very specific pain of ego-abnegation becomes less traumatic by the acquisition of a greater universal openness.

The locating of one's own personal pain within the universal pain of existence makes one's subjective ego pain bearable both with the diminishment of the ego and with the objective proportionalization of personal suffering within universal suffering. This deeper objective pain of the psyche, unlike ego pain, is not debilitating, for it has been brought about by a receptivity. At this point of universal openness, not only is the entire subject matter of psychomoralitics shifted away from the therapant's self, but the very orientation of the therapant is shifted away from himself as well.

A person coming from a locus in the ego can endure little psychomoral pain in comparison to a person coming from a locus in the psyche. As a person advances upon the psychomoralitic path of well-being and encounters reality from the psyche, he peacefully enters into the full depths of personal, universal, and existential sorrow. In doing so, a person enters into the full summits of joy as well; indeed, he enters into the fullness of human being.

Causing Disquietude Amongst the Coping

Disquietude is a prerequisite disposition for psychomoralitic endeavors. Thus disquietude needs to be instilled in those who come to psychomoralitics in the coping state. While most come to psychomoralitics because they are not coping and hence must only have the source of their disquietude uncovered, others (such as a clinician-in-training or the spouse[130] of a person not coping)

---

130 This instillation of disquietude in a spouse or other significant family member or friend and that person's subsequent entering into psychomoralitics is not only the best way to facilitate change in the primary therapant, but in the family member or friend himself, which is a good in itself.

may be called to voluntarily come out of their coping state by the psychomoralitic process. So too, all therapants have times when they slip into a certain *status quo* common coping, when the onslaught of impacting reality is not so urgent. However, it is the clinician's job to help therapant's in such a coping state to freely choose to forgo coping and breach the defenses of a selective reality. Thus such a coping therapant who comes into a session coping, may leave the session feeling worse! Yet hopefully he will leave as well with a deep abiding peace that will sustain him throughout the vicissitudes of the interim between sessions, and beyond.

In the coping state, the art of psychomoralitics is the variable process of persuading a therapant to say *yes* to impacting reality and thus awaken from an existential somnolence and an egoistic ethos. In order to facilitate the psychomoralitic moment where *yes* can be issued, a psychomoralist must be able to locate and prudently "push the buttons" of a therapant's unique coping mechanisms so as to help the therapant transcend them to the depths of the ego they protect. In doing so, a therapant is encouraged to acquire a sense of urgency and disgust with his enslavement to these coping mechanisms and his fear of ego abnegation and the ensuing ego passions.

Psychomoralitics holds that these metaphorical buttons may be located in different areas and manifest under a sundry of symptoms, but are all eventually wired to the ego. To apply psychomoralitics persuasion, a clinician must find these buttons, these defenses, which entails finding within a therapant the motivational keys that will trigger a sense of urgency. The circular dynamics of psychomoralitics is seen in the root motivational keys being existential concerns, such as death and meaninglessness, and the concomitant humiliation and sorrow of suffering, death, and annihilation/damnation that need to be progressively unmasked. This in effect brings the therapeutic process back to the beginning existential area of receiving-the-real. With the experiencing of the good embraced, the clinician then begins the process again, on a deeper level, where the therapant is persuaded to be totally receptive on an existential level and again, convinced that it is good to say *yes* to impacting reality and that it is a good dynamic that he is experiencing psychomorally.

Psychomoralitic intervention, then, requires that the psychomoralist effectively challenge the therapant to embrace his discontentment and his failure to live up to his human vocation as a seeker of truth and doer of good. The Basque poet-philosopher Miguel de Unamuno (1905) wrote:

> There are small minds who assert that it is better to be a contented pig than an unhappy human being. But he who has once tasted the flavor of humanity, he will—even in profound misery—prefer the unhappiness of man to the contentment of the pig. It is well, therefore to cause disquietude in human souls and to enkindle in them a mighty yearning.[131]

---

131 Reinhardt, K. F. *The Existentialist Revolt: The Main Themes and Phases of Existentialism*. Alternative translation (pg. 234); Milwaukee: Bruce Publishing (1952).

A small mind, that is a soul encrusted with coping mechanisms and fears, is one not open to the fullness of reality, and thus not in possession of peace, not growing in essential well-being, nor able to experience full human flourishing. "To cause [or more aptly uncover] disquietude in human souls and to enkindle in them a mighty yearning" is essential to the psychomoralitic process. Again, facilitating such a "disquietude" and "mighty yearning" is a psychomoralitic goal when dealing with those in a state of myopic, lukewarm, and omissive coping. Psychomoralitic disquietude is the awareness of one's inner wretchedness, which leads one to recognize both the evil within and the evil without. Psychomoralitic yearning is the awareness of reality, which leads one to lovingly choose and courageously champion that reality, truth, and good. Thus this psychomoralitic disquietude and yearning is also essential to the fulfillment of the human vocation as a seeker of the real and the true, and doer of the subsequent good. Again, Josef Pieper (1889) wrote:

> For life to be truly human it seems indispensable that... [one accept] the challenge, disturbing yet fruitful, coming from the world's ultimate reality.[132]

Psychomoralitic disquietude and yearning, disturbing yet fruitful, is essential for the flourishing of the human spirit and to the breaking of all the psychomoral fetters that might quash and enslave that spirit. The first fetters to be broken are the inner psychomoral defensive fears and pervasive interpersonal dysfunction. But once these psychomoral fetters are broken, a

---

132 *Ibid.*

person gains as well the humility, prophetic insight, and zealous courage to break free from the fetters of coercive and enslaving sociopolitical structures, technarcistic anesthetizations, and from the dehumanizing prescriptions of the mental health system itself.

12. R.E.V.E.R.E.

PSYCHOMORALITICS UNIQUELY PLUMMETS the sacrosanct realm of the human person, and hence the depths of human suffering and joy. As such, a psychomoralist or psychomoral mentor must possess the very highest of skills in regards to rapport and empathy. So too, for the psychomoral clinician to authentically encounter the therapant he must come from the depths of his own psyche, thus transcending his own superficiality and egoistic good. Psychomoralitics uses the apt acronym *R.E.V.E.R.E.* to outline its requisite clinical skills and dispositions, for nothing less than reverential treatment is called for from those who are invited to enter into the soul-deep drama of another human person's existence.

R.E.V.E.R.E. stands for *Revering, Encountering, Varying, Educating, Relinquishing,* and *Encouraging*. These qualities describe the key goals and dispositions that should be ever present in the psychomoralitic process. They apply not only to the disposition of the clinician but should pervade the entire clinical milieu as well, including the comportment of staff and the therapants.

Revering

Both in name, chronology, and pervasiveness, *revering* is the flagship of R.E.V.E.R.E. A clinician's psychomoral presence includes a reverence manifested in a bearing and disposition that is proper to the solemnity of psychomoralitics. Again, the solemnity of psychomoralitics is due to its plummeting of the innermost depths of a therapant's sacrosanct soul and very existence. The clinician's reverential bearing and disposition witnesses to the therapant of this solemn nature of psychomoralitics and models as well for the therapant the proper bearing and disposition toward the drama of one's existence and human existence in general.

Because psychomoralitics entails a clinician helping a therapant suffer well, it is a very delicate, precious, and reverential process. Not only must the therapant's entering into suffering be personally revered by the clinician in session, but the entire psychomoralitic process and clinical cultural milieu should reflect this reverence. In more reverential pastimes, outside of hospitals there were actual street signs that read, *"Quiet: Hospital Zone."* Inside the hospital, the staff and visitors comported themselves with a certain bearing that recognized the intensified human drama that was unfolding in their midst. This human drama is the human drama of hope, birth, renewed life, and joy; and it is the human drama of fear, suffering, death, and sorrow. Today, what with modern medicine's technological nature and ensuing technarcistic ethos, this drama is not appreciated as it should be in medical settings, thus all the more reason for its appreciation and implementation in the psychomoralitic setting.

A clinician's reverential bearing and disposition is also in regards to the person of the therapant. The clinician revers the therapant in his human nature, that is, as a being whose vocation is that of a seeker of truth and beatitude, and a doer of good, and as one that must learn to suffer-well so as to fulfill this vocation. But this reverential attitude towards the therapant is not humanistic psychology's *"unconditional positive regard"*[133] of the therapant's pseudo-self. Indeed, the psychomoral clinician does not revere the pseudo-self of the therapant but seeks its demise; and this is all the more reason to proceed with reverence.

Mental health psychotherapy, especially the humanistic and person-centered therapies, enshrines the subjective point of view and facilitates egocentrism. Such theories increase the already inherent danger in psychotherapy to fixate on the therapant and thus produce the iatrogenic (i.e., clinically created) phenomenon of *psychovitiation (i.e.,*harm caused by mental health interventions) that not only increases psychomoral mal-being, but that even exacerbates and/or creates the symptoms classified as mental illness.

This inherent danger of egocentric fixation is present even in psychomoralitics, which must necessarily utilize the subjective point of view of a therapant to remedy it effectively, and is necessarily focused on the therapant in an attempt to have him

---

133 Carl Rogers (1902 – 1987).

confront his own ego-centrism. In that psychomoralitics brings good out of bad, that which did or did not take place in a therapant's upbringing, the world, at least during the session, once again revolves around the therapant, just as it does the child or adolescent. But in psychomoralitics this self-absorption leads not to the enhancement of the pseudo-self but to its abnegation.

There inevitably comes a time when this subjective and egocentric orientation of intervention begins to bring in diminishing returns, when the narcissism of a therapy revolving around oneself and one's thoughts and passions is only delaying growth and becomes part of the problem. It then becomes necessary for the therapant to reorient himself from a fixation on self to an openness to reality and a focus on truth. Once the clinician discerns that enough therapeutic rapport and leverage has been gained, he should begin to facilitate this reorientation by challenging the therapant's subjective ego-centrism. Needless to say, an overindulgence of a therapant's ego-centrism early on only makes this transition more difficult.

The psychomoral clinician reveres that within the therapant that transcends the therapant's pseudo-self. This transcendent element is the psyche, or is at least found in the psyche, and may aptly be termed the *imago Dei*. This *image of God* is by definition mysterious, but at leastwise that which makes a human person a human person: a being able to assent to truth and love the good. Indeed, because this *imago Dei* transcends the pseudo-self of the person, it is what is somehow truly unique about the person.

But let it suffice to say in a non-theological work that the inner unlimited depths of a person are beyond measurement and thus are properly held in reverential appreciation. In the psychomoralitic process the clinician knows well the therapant; and maybe knows the therapant better than anyone else. However, no matter the knowledge gained of the therapant, the therapant in his essence must always be seen as an unfathomable mystery that infinitely transcends all that can be known about him. The infinitely transcending mystery of the human person is the locus of a clinician's revering of the therapant.

A most important ramification of holding the revered element of a person as having a locus beyond the specifics of the person—and most importantly the pseudo-self—is that in doing so *that which commands reverence in a person can never be diminished or taken away*, no matter the physical, psychological, moral, or social/political/juridical state of the particular person. Thus neither doctor, nor judge, nor mob, nor State can alter this element to be revered, indeed held in awe, in each human person.

A reverent clinical disposition—from clinician to clinical milieu to the therapant—is a psychomoralitic prerequisite. Again, in the psychomoralitic process one encounters the human person in his vulnerable inner being, a place of awe and mystery. This moral realm entails that which is not dissectible and not quantifiable. To only view it as such is to brutalize it. Not only must the psychomoral clinician always *revere* the non-quantifiable mystery of the therapant, and thus the psychomoralitic process itself, but the clinical setting too must reflect this reverence. This quality of reverence is not only the proper psychomoralitic milieu but the most efficacious as well. Such a reverent milieu facilitates a therapant's trust that they are valued in the depth of their being. For a reverential disposition is contrary to superficiality, but rather facilitates an authentic encounter. [134]

Encountering

The best way to assure a clinician's proper reverential disposition is for the clinician to be simultaneously undergoing psychomoralitics. Indeed, this is to be expected of the clinician since psychomoralitics is a lifelong process that formal sessions inculcate one with but does not end when they end. The deepest psychomoralitics takes place outside of and beyond the end of formal sessions. For psychomoralitics deals with the essence of life. When a clinician is able to be gratefully receptive and revere the dramatic essence of his own life he will revere the dramatic

---

134 In keeping with the solemn and sublime nature of the psychomoralitic process and to facilitate its efficacy, clinical policy should advise therapant's and others to comport themselves in a befitting manner while at the clinical site. For instance, cellphones and electronics should be silenced. Standards of dress are one of the easiest ways to facilitate external comportment and interior disposition. While clinicians and staff should always dress professionally, therapant's themselves should also be reminded to do so, so as to greater appreciate the solemnity of the psychotherapeutic process. A therapant who from the first moment of entering the clinic door experiences a reverential milieu in which he is encountered authentically, will already leave behind much of the superficiality and defensive distractions of the world. Indeed, therapants should be counseled to prepare even before their appointment with some quiet and reflective time.

essence of all human existence and thus the dramatic essence of his therapant's life.

The clinician's simultaneous undergoing of psychomoralitic self-abnegation and subsequent increased openness to reality with the therapant is also the means of authentically encountering the therapant at the deepest existential level. This deepest encounter requires both the clinician and the therapant to come from the depths of the psyche, but it is the clinician who facilitates this in the therapant by being first present from his own existential depths. To do so does not mean that the clinician self-discloses particular facts about himself, much less does it mean giving free reign to the ego or pseudo-self. Rather it means that the clinician is psychomorally present in the depths of his being. This authentic psychomoral presence is exactly what needs to be modeled for the therapant, for it transcends defenses and the ego, which is the crux of psychomoralitics. Eventually for the therapant himself, the essential content of psychomoralitics becomes not so much about the particulars of his life but of the lasting impact these particulars have had upon him and the allowance of this impact to abnegate the ego and pierce the psyche.[135]

---

135 Psychomoral groups are conducted in accord with these principles of authentic moral presence. Thus the emphasis is not on the particulars of one's life cathartically expressed (i.e., *spilled and spelled out*) to others, nor to ego interaction or reaction. Rather psychomoral groups are ordered to therapants being present from the depths of their being in transcendence of both the particulars of impacting reality and ego defenses.

For the clinician to initiate the movement toward this *bilateral existential encounter,* he must from his depths begin encountering the subjective experience of the therapant, which initially includes, and even predominately, strong ego passions. For the subjective experience, even if inappropriate, is nonetheless the experienced reality of the therapant. In the encounter of a therapant at this stage the clinician must be so disposed that his own ego and defenses are not effectively triggered by those of the therapant. This disposition requires the clinician to be receptive to the impacting reality of the therapant's ego passions and defenses. This allows the clinician to avoid reacting from his own ego, but rather to respond from his psyche in an empathetic, sorrowful, and non-defensive (even if directive) manner. In doing so, not only is the clinician experiencing ego-abnegation but modeling for the therapant the proper disposition of receptivity to impacting reality.

Often a therapant's ego defenses and passions are reactions to another person's vicious ego defenses and passion against them. In projection, the therapant may then relate to the clinician in the same manner. This is the golden opportunity for the clinician to show *in vivo* the therapant how he need not react out of the ego and thus avoid the *sinergy*[136] of escalating ego's in conflict, but rather the allowance of ego-abnegation which will free the therapant from the past.

---

136 Sinergy: A psychomoralitic term for a vicious and increasing *synergy* between egos.

Paradoxically enough, the term *leisure* aptly describes the clinician's mode of existential operation in psychomoralitics. While having to be cognizant of clinical evaluation, time, notes, etc, the clinician must also maintain a leisurely presence. Leisure here defined is "being in the moment and being in the presence of oneself or another." This entails then being undistractedly[137] in the moment, in the now, in the real. A clinician then is called to an attitude of peaceful receptivity, saying *yes* first to the impacting reality of his own personal life, then to universal impacting reality, and finally to the impacting reality of his therapant. Thus these impacting realities—personal, universal, and of the therapant—should commingle harmoniously within the clinician as he conducts psychomoralitics. The clinician with a leisurely psychomoralitic implementation is authentic, long-suffering, and deep.

Varying

In psychomoralitics the clinician is required to not only observe but to *empathetically encounter* the therapant in the essence of his being. In this empathetic encounter, not only is true rapport established but subtle qualitative clues that help the art of psychomoralitics are garnered. The clinical navigation of the non-

---

137 Thus recreation is often not truly leisurely but distracting. Though some forms of recreation produce an intensity of experience that requires complete focus (such as rock climbing)m, the focus is myopic (even if the reality of a cliff and the existential moment). The leisure spoken of here is not a focused intensity on one aspect of reality that excludes all else, but rather an openness to all reality.

quantifiable is necessary because, though the fundamental psychomoral topography common to all people can be known, in each therapant it is uniquely strewn with defenses and possible avenues of approach. So too, the psychomoral interior of the human person is not discernible by the glaring light of quantification, rather it is in the twilight, and even at times darkness, of the non-quantifiable. Each person is a mystery, not because the topography is not known, but because ultimately that topography gives way to the unfathomable expanse of the psyche.

Psychomoralitics is existential (i.e., concerned with being) both in its deductive scientific principles and its inductive psychotherapeutic art. Thus a psychomoral clinician, though moored to deductive, normative, and objective truths, must be able to enter into the subjective experiences of the therapant. All clinical sciences utilize some inductive reasoning or phenomenological observation to discover particular symptomology and thus come to diagnostic conclusions. In addition to variable subjective perceptions, each therapant is unique in his inherent intellectual, psychological and physical abilities and disabilities; in his domestic, social, and personal history; in his educational, real-world background; and a myriad of other variables.

The existential encounter of a therapant's subjective and objective experiential reality facilitates the development of a varying individualized treatment plan. Each therapant is unique, each has an inherent lesson plan that the formal lesson plan needs to be adapted to. Thus treatment plans that are too rigid can impede the efficacy of psychomoralitics. While following a model treatment plan outline, the content and even the outline itself can vary greatly.

So too treatment plans must be open to modification during the course of psychomoralitics. Events will continue to occur in the therapant's life that can be used psychomoralitically. This incorporation of real time events is ordered toward both psychomoralitic receptivity to impacting reality as well as substantive life changes. Such life changes can be vocational, relational, social, or familial. Sometimes such changes are foisted upon a therapant from outside himself and sometimes they come from the therapant himself. The therapant's successful psychomoral change of his character is manifested in tangible choices and occurrences. Even external changes foisted upon a therapant are often due to his characterological change, since when he changes, the dysfunctional homeostasis of his relations with others is disrupted.

Educational

The educational element of psychomoralitics requires that the clinician convince the therapant of both the truth of the conceptualization and the truth of its manifestation in his life. This is encountering the real in the mode of truth. The trust of the therapant should be in psychomoralitics primarily, and secondarily in the therapist. This means a therapant should take notes and be an active learner, especially during the early part, formally known as the pedagogical preface.

As therapy progresses a clinician should employ the Socratic method[138] more and more. This method elicits from the therapant the truth about reality, about the psychomoral conceptualization, and about himself. This Socratic eliciting is done via questions. At times questions will need to be somewhat leading if the therapant is having difficulty. The therapant's ability to answer the question and even frame the question himself is an indication that he has made the psychomoral conceptualization his own. This is crucial since the therapant must be able to apply the principles of psychomoralitics on a constant and habitual basis throughout his day and life.

Relinquishing

An effective psychomoral clinician must relinquish all egoistic neediness in the psychomoralitic process. Clinician's will vary in their degree of egoistic neediness and this neediness will also vary as each clinician goes through his own personal vicissitudes. But relinquishing egoistic neediness does not mean that a clinician must fake it or be superficial, for this would be

---

138 The Socratic method is a form of inquiry and discussion between individuals, based on asking and answering questions to stimulate critical thinking and to illuminate ideas. It is a dialectical method, often involving a discussion in which the defense of one point of view is questioned; one participant may lead another to contradict themselves in some way, thus weakening the defender's point.

very detrimental to efficacious psychomoralitics. Such superficiality would also be detrimental to the clinician since it would be a stressful ego coping mechanism against the fullness of reality.

Rather, a psychomoral clinician transcends his egoistic neediness by allowing his ego to feel the full brunt of humiliation. Egoistic neediness is relinquished by saying *yes* to one's humiliations. This hurt may be in the form of relational poverty, that is, pain in regards to people (or the lack thereof) one is intimate with. It may come in the form of threats to one's security: physically, professionally, socially, familially, or existentially. But in any case, the clinician is called to continue the psychomoralitic process which he has provenly undergone during his clinical training.

The psychomoral clinician must relinquish as well the desire to be accepted by his therapants. Rather, the clinician seeks first and foremost that the psychomoral conceptualization is accepted Indeed, if the clinician is himself embracing the conceptualization, then he is in his person giving the therapant what is required. The possibility that a therapant will reject psychomoralitics is increased by a myriad of voices, including those of mainstream psychology, proposing a discordant and often diametrically opposed conceptualization that is an easier way and a way out of the soul-deep psychomoralitic process. Psychomoralitics can be seen as "surgery" in contrast to the "placebo elixir" proffered by psychotherapists or the numbing drugs proffered by psychiatrists. And just like the surgery of yesterday, psychomoralitics will be initially rejected in favor of popular mental health quackery.

A therapant or other "interested" parties—be these family, friends, or the mental health system itself—unwilling to enter into or accept psychomoralitics may lead to the demonizing of the clinician. Such demonizing is necessary, for if the therapant (or whoever) is right in rejecting psychomoralitics, the psychomoralist must be wrong. But again this is an intrinsic part of psychomoralitics and the promulgating of psychomoralitics, and a clinician must be open to ego-abnegation and sorrow of the psyche for the good of his therapant and his own good as well.

The psychomoral clinician must also be willing to relinquish the active psychomoralitic relationship itself when the time has come. This can be done by gradually facilitating the therapant's relinquishing of that relationship. In this regard the psychomoralist should facilitate the replacement of his role, if possible, by that of a spouse or good friend who is also upon the psychomoralitic path, but if not by a change in general lifestyle. A very common transfer from formal psychomoralitics (though the dynamic continues through life), is that of immersion in the study of philosophical and/or theological knowledge accessible via books, etc., that is congruent with the psychomoral conceptualization and facilitates its continued application.

Encouraging

Relinquishing acceptance, or being unafraid of rejection, is crucial if a clinician is to challenge and encourage his therapants to embrace the fullness of psychomoralitic transformation. This again is premised on the view that those suffering with dominating ego-reactivity (and sometimes the symptomologies known as mental disorder) should not try to achieve "normalcy." Indeed, they will most likely fail in the attempt, if normalcy is the state of coping, that is, being only selectively open to reality. Rather those upon the psychomoralitic path of human flourishing are called to a greater openness to reality than normal.

Indeed, a clinician assumes some culpability for the future of his therapants or even those his therapants influence—such as their children—if because of his own fear of rejection or conflict he avoids dealing with "touchy subjects" or does not present a challenge for the therapant to embrace an heroic future that would upset a coping equilibrium that may have set in to the psychomoralitic process itself. A therapant should leave formal psychomoralitic sessions with a perpetual ego discontentment, but still with an abiding psyche peace: to saying *yes* to ever greater impacting reality; to ever greater ego-abnegation; to ever greater psychic openness; and to ever greater sorrow and joy.

To so challenge a therapant is the duty of the psychomoral clinician. The psychomoral clinician courageously encourages a therapant to go where even he may fear to go. Though done prudently, gradually, and artfully so as to best facilitate the therapant's acceptance, such challenging encouragement nonetheless will always entail the risk of the therapant's rejection of psychomoralitics, but more likely of the clinician himself. But courage is fueled by loving something more than one's egoistic self. For the psychomoral clinician, let his courage be fueled by a love of being, of reality, of truth, and of the good, and let it be specifically fueled by a reverential love of the deepest essence of his therapant.

APPENDIX A:
THE CRUCIAL HUMAN VOCATIONS

THE HUMAN PERSON MUST BE ENCOUNTERED and treated holistically to avoid brutalization and harm to some aspect of his personhood. A holistic approach is especially urgent when intervening in the depths of the soul to remedy ego-reactivity and mal-being. For such an intervention to be holistic and integral, it must treat or take into account the four essential human vocations.

Psychomoralitics uniquely addresses the soul-deep psychomoral realm as well as the incarnational realm of mortality and gender. The formation and actualization of these first two vocations takes place primarily within the realm of the familial third vocation, which itself exists within, and is properly facilitated by, the realm of the sociopolitical fourth vocation. A therapant will only achieve deep characterological change when he courageously interacts with others and his milieu.

True and deep remedying of mal-being and achieving of well-being will always have personal, familial, and societal ramifications. Sometimes even prophetic ramifications. However, when a person is taken as an isolated individual "patient" or "client," change remains clinical and necessarily limited.

1) *Psychomoral Vocation*

The psychomoral vocation entails the human person's call as a seeker of truth and good and beatitude: a rational-volitional being made in *imago Dei* (i.e., God's image). Here the psychomoral development of the human person is addressed, promoted, and, if necessary, treated according to the timeless Thomistic anthropology of the Church that is found in Psychomoralitics.

2) *Incarnational Vocation*

The incarnational vocation entails the human person's call as an *imago Dei* enfleshed. Here man's existential vocation as a mortal being in this "valley of tears" and his human incarnational status as either male or female is explicated and embraced in accord with philosophical truth and physiological givens.

3) *Familial Vocation*

The familial vocation is based on God-given gender and its ensuing dynamics, especially as per wife-mother and husband-father. Via the familial vocation and in the familial realm, both the preceding psychomoralitic and incarnational vocations unfold essentially. So too, the following fourth vocation is ordered to the familial realm. Thus the family is properly given primacy in the education and formation of the human person.

4) Sociopolitical Vocation

The sociopolitical vocation is as a member of the community of families and the secular political body via personhood and family. The sociopolitical is properly ordered toward the well-being of the individual and the family. The sociopolitical order, according to the principles of subsidiarity, begins with the grassroots community of families and extends therefrom.

Appendix B:

Technarcistic Man

Today's Technarcistic Man is mired in a relativistic pride that leads him to expect, and even delusionally imagine, that reality conforms to his subjective desires. Whereas previous editions of Man, though they may not always have liked reality, nonetheless knew that they had to conform to it.

Technological artifice and material abundance have brought about today's Technarcistic Man and his many maladies. Today's Technarcistic Man has ample means to anesthetize himself to reality, which effects an unawareness or certain blindness in regards to reality, natural law, and thus even gender. The pathogenesis of this unawareness or blindness is a person becoming myopically fixated on himself and his subjective good —most characteristically, even to the point of being addicted to his subjective pleasure and entertainment.

The basis of this blindness is a narcissism where the contemporary person no longer even recognizes, or at least fully appreciates, that his contingency is the most radical principle of his creaturely human existence.

> "[The rational creature] has a share of the eternal reason, whereby it has a natural inclination to its proper act and end, and this participation of the

eternal law in the rational creature is called the
natural law." (I-II q91, a2)

Though Aquinas does not explicate this, the rational
creature's essential proper act and end is to give glory to God,
and this must begin by saying "yes" to God being God and the
creature not being God. Thus, as is evidenced in the creation
account, adhering to and not rebelling against the essential reality
that *God is God and the creature is not,* is the first principle of
natural law.

Contingency is the most radical principle of human existence
because it is the principle of *not having to exist.* When one's
contingency is realized a person knows he does not have to exist; he
knows reality is not about himself, not centered around himself; he
knows God is God and he is not. Even for many theists today, in
practice, God exists *for them*: He exists to answer prayers, to make one
happy, to make life bearable. But this is tantamount to a practical
atheism, for if God exists for man, then God really isn't God, but
rather a genie in a bottle. In any case, to be anesthetized and blinded
to this principle of one's contingency, to the fact that one essentially
exists for God, entails not accepting or realizing one's existential
realities.

The second reason for technarcism is the advancement of
totalitarian ideological and political agendas. These agendas—be their
origins in secularism, materialism capitalism, socialism, or
communism—are essentially *anti-God,* for a viable God limits their
authority and power. Being essentially anti-God, these ideologies end

up denying even the most elementary truths of reality and creation; and necessarily so, since God is the author and source of reality.

APPENDIX C:
INTRA-PROFESSIONAL CONDEMNATIONS

Note Well: In the following, and very far from exhaustive, compilation of condemnatory statements, only authorities from within the Mental Health Profession itself are cited. It is impossible to keep all of the experts on the reservation at all times. However, it is possible to marginalize those who issue dissenting statements. Nonetheless, the doctors cited below either in a moment of unguarded honesty, or in a fit of frustration at their ineffectuality, or as a result of heartfelt repentance for the harm they have promulgated, have exposed the mental health profession for what it is: a fraudulent scam, an ineffectual and deadly treatment, and an invalid science. All of the mental health professions are DSM disciplines, that is, they have as their foundational document the scientifically invalid and intra-professionally repudiated Diagnostic & Statistical Manual that is referenced below. Finally, psychiatrists, who are cited below, are the ultimate authorities in the mental health system, having formed an unholy alliance with the State, pharmaceutical, insurance complex.

Ψ

"All models of psychotherapy, including cognitive behavior therapy, may be equally unsound scientifically but they energize the therapists and provide useful fictions to activate the patients to lead somewhat more satisfactory lives." *American Journal of Psychiatry;*

Cognitive Behavior Therapy for Depression? G. Parker, et al., citing Stravynski & Greenberg: *The psychological management of depression. Acta Psychiatr Scand* 1992; Pub. online: May 01, 2003.

~~~~~~~

As per the author of the *Diagnostic and Statistical Manual III*, which is the very "bible" of the mental health profession, *"To say that we've solved the reliability problem is just not true...if you're in a situation with a general clinician it's certainly not very good. There's still a real problem, and it's not clear how to solve the problem." American Psychiatric Association's task force of Diagnostic and Statistical Manual of Mental Disorders, 3r;d Author: Spitzer, R., The New Yorker's Annals of Medicine Jan, 3, 2005.*

~~~~~~~

That the FDA requires a "black box" label on all antidepressants warning of the possibility that ingestion of these psychotropics will induce suicide. And that, *"Nearly all patients who remain on these chemical agents[i.e., psychotropics] for many years will develop some symptoms of CBI [Chronic Brain Injury]. . . . Each of these reactions can worsen the individual's mental condition and can result in suicidality, violence, and other forms of extreme abnormal behavior." International Journal of Risk & Safety in Medicine,* 23: 193-200; P.R. Breggin, 2011, Psychiatrist, *Psychiatric drug induced Chronic Brain Impairment.*

~~~~~~~

Those diagnosed with schizophrenia but left unmedicated with psychotropics *"have a significant better global functioning than those on antipsychotics,"*and have a much higher recovery rate (40% vs. 5%) as well. M. Harrow, Psychiatrist, *American Psychiatric Association* Presentation, 2008.

"We do not know the causes [of any mental illness]. We don't have the methods of 'curing' these illnesses yet." R. Cowdry, Psychiatrist, Director 1995 *National Institute of Mental Health*

~~~~~~~

"The time when psychiatrists considered that they could cure the mentally ill is gone." N. Satorius, Psychiatrist, President 1994 *World Psychiatric Association*

~~~~~~~

"'Mental illness' is terribly misleading because the 'mental disorders' we diagnose are no more than descriptions of what clinicians observe people do or say, not at all well established diseases." Allen Frances, Psychiatrist and former DSM-IV Task Force Chairman, 2015

~~~~~~~

"While DSM has been described as a 'Bible' for the field, it is, at best, a dictionary…. The weakness is its lack of validity. Unlike our definitions of ischemic heart disease, lymphoma, or AIDS, the DSM diagnoses are based on a consensus about clusters of clinical symptoms, not any objective laboratory measure. In the rest of medicine, this would be equivalent to creating diagnostic systems based on the nature of chest pain or the quality of fever." — Thomas Insel, Director of the *National Institute of Mental Health.*

~~~~~~~

"There are no objective tests in psychiatry, no X-ray, laboratory, or exam finding that says definitively that someone does or does not have a mental disorder." "There is no definition of a mental disorder. It's bull—. I mean, you just can't define it." — Allen

Frances, Psychiatrist and former *DSM-IV Task Force* Chairman.

~~~~~~~

"Virtually anyone at any given time can meet the criteria for bipolar disorder or ADHD. Anyone. And the problem is everyone diagnosed with even one of these 'illnesses' triggers the pill dispenser." — Stefan Kruszewski, Psychiatrist

~~~~~~~

While there has been "no shortage of alleged biochemical explanations for psychiatric conditions…not one has been proven. Quite the contrary. In every instance where such an imbalance was thought to have been found, it was later proven false." — Joseph Glenmullen, Psychiatrist, Harvard Medical School

~~~~~~~

"The theories are held on to not only because there is nothing else to take their place, but also because they are useful in promoting drug treatment." — Elliott Valenstein Ph.D., author of *Blaming the Brain*

~~~~~~~

"DSM IV is the fabrication upon which psychiatry seeks acceptance by medicine in general. Insiders know it is more a political than scientific document. To its credit it says so — although its brief apologia is rarely noted. DSM IV has become a bible and a money making best seller — its major failings notwithstanding. It confines and defines practice, some take it seriously, others more realistically. It is the way to get paid. Diagnostic reliability is easy to attain for research projects. The issue is what do the categories tell us? Do they in fact accurately represent the person with a problem? They don't, and can't, because there are no external validating criteria for psychiatric diagnoses." Loren Mosher, Psychiatrist, former Chief of NIMH's *Center for Studies of Schizophrenia,* head of Schizophrenia Research, *National Institute of Mental health*

~~~~~~~

"We do not have an independent, valid test for ADHD, and there are no data to indicate ADHD is due to a brain malfunction." — Final statement of the panel from the *National Institutes of Health Consensus Conference* on ADHD

~~~~~~~

"The way things get into the DSM is not based on blood test or brain scan or physical findings. It's based on descriptions of behavior. And that's what the whole psychiatry system is." — Colin Ross, Psychiatrist

~~~~~~~

"Despite more than two hundred years of intensive research, no commonly diagnosed psychiatric disorders have proven to be either genetic or biological in origin, including schizophrenia, major depression, manic-depressive disorder, the various anxiety disorders, and childhood disorders such as attention-deficit hyperactivity. At present there are no known biochemical imbalances in the brain of typical psychiatric patients—until they are given psychiatric drugs."

"In reality, psychiatric diagnosing is a kind of spiritual profiling that can destroy lives and frequently does. . . . Psychiatry has never been driven by science. They have no biological or genetic basis for these illnesses and the National Institutes of Mental Health are totally committed to the pharmacological line. ... There is a great deal of scientific evidence that stimulants cause brain damage with long-term use, yet there is no evidence that these mental illnesses, such as ADHD, exist." — Peter Breggin, Psychiatrist

~~~~~~~

"No claim for a gene for a psychiatric condition has stood the test of time, in spite of popular misinformation." — Joseph Glenmullen, Psychiatrist, *Harvard Medical School*

~~~~~~~

"... modern psychiatry has yet to convincingly prove the genetic/biologic cause of any single mental illness...Patients [have] been diagnosed with 'chemical imbalances' despite the fact that no test exists to support such a claim, and...there is no real conception of what a correct chemical balance would look like." — David Kaiser, Psychiatrist

~~~~~~~

"There's no biological imbalance. When people come to me and they say, 'I have a biochemical imbalance,' I say, 'Show me your lab tests.' There are no lab tests. So what's the biochemical imbalance?" — Ron Leifer, Psychiatrist

~~~~~~~

"All psychiatrists have in common that when they are caught on camera or on microphone, they cower and admit that there are no such things as chemical imbalances/diseases, or examinations or tests for them. What they do in practice, lying in every instance, abrogating [revoking] the informed consent right of every patient and poisoning them in the name of 'treatment' is nothing short of criminal." — Fred Baughman Jr., Pediatric Neurologist

~~~~~~~

"It has occurred to me with forcible irony that psychiatry has quite literally lost its mind, and along with it the minds of the patients they are presumably supposed to care for."

"Psychiatry [makes]... unproven claims that depression, bipolar illness, anxiety, alcoholism and a host of other disorders are in fact primarily biologic and probably genetic in origin...This kind of faith in science and progress is staggering, not to mention naïve and perhaps delusional." — David Kaiser, psychiatrist

~~~~~~~

"In short, the whole business of creating psychiatric categories of 'disease,' formalizing them with consensus, and subsequently ascribing diagnostic codes to them, which in turn leads to their use for insurance billing, is nothing but an extended racket furnishing psychiatry a pseudo-scientific aura. The perpetrators are, of course, feeding at the public trough." — Dr. Thomas Dorman, internist and member of the *Royal College of Physicians of the UK*

~~~~~~~

"I believe, until the public and psychiatry itself see that DSM labels are not only useless as medical 'diagnoses' but also have the potential to do great harm—particularly when they are used as means to deny individual freedoms, or as weapons by

psychiatrists acting as hired guns for the legal system." — Sydney
Walker III, psychiatrist

~~~~~~~

"No biochemical, neurological, or genetic markers have been
found for Attention Deficit Disorder, Oppositional Defiant
Disorder, Depression, Schizophrenia, anxiety, compulsive alcohol
and drug abuse, overeating, gambling or any other so-called
mental illness, disease, or disorder." — Bruce Levine, Ph.D.,
psychologist and author of *Commonsense Rebellion*

~~~~~~~

"Unlike medical diagnoses that convey a probable cause,
appropriate treatment and likely prognosis, the disorders listed in
DSM-IV [and ICD-10] are terms arrived at through peer
consensus." — Tana Dineen Ph.D., psychologist.

~~~~~~~

"There is no blood or other biological test to ascertain the
presence or absence of a mental illness, as there is for most bodily
diseases.

"No behavior or misbehavior is a disease or can be a disease.
That's not what diseases are. Diseases are malfunctions of the
human body, of the heart, the liver, the kidney, the brain. Typhoid
fever is a disease. Spring fever is not a disease; it is a figure of
speech, a metaphoric disease. All mental diseases are metaphoric
diseases, misrepresented as real diseases and mistaken for real
diseases."

"It is not science. It's politics and economics. That's what psychiatry
is: politics and economics. Behavior control, it is not science, it is not

medicine." — Thomas Szasz, Professor of Psychiatry Emeritus at the *State University of New York Health Science Center.*

APPENDIX D:
A RESIGNATION LETTER

(A resignation letter from an "old-school" psychologist, and formerly very staunch member of the American Psychological Association, that was sent to APA President Alan Kazdin and the APA Council of Representatives on February 7, 2008.)

Alan E. Kazdin, Ph.D.
President
American Psychological Association
750 First Street, NE
Washington, DC 20002-4242

Dear Alan,

With sadness I write to resign from the American Psychological Association. My respect and affection for the members, along with my 29 year history with APA, make this a hard and reluctant step. Chairing the Ethics Committee, holding fellow status in 9 divisions, and receiving the APA Award for Distinguished Contributions to Public Service, the Division 12

Award for Distinguished Professional Contributions to Clinical Psychology, and the Division 42 Award for Mentoring reflect a few chapters in my APA history.

I respectfully disagree with decisive changes that APA has made in its ethical stance during the past 6+ years. These changes moved APA far from its ethical foundation, historic traditions, and basic values, and beyond what I can in good conscience support with my membership. I would like to note two examples of disagreement. First, the years since 9-11 brought concern over psychologists' work that affects detainees. APA has stressed psychologists' "vital role" regarding "the use of ethical interrogations to safeguard the welfare of detainees" and ways that psychologists "help advance the cause of detainee welfare and humane treatment." Yet in its ethics code, APA chose not to recognize any humane treatment requirements governing psychologists' work with detainees as enforceable standards....

My second area of disagreement concerns the ethics code that Council adopted August 21, 2002 (which took effect June 1, 2003). The 2002 code echoes the earlier code in setting forth the following enforceable standard: "If psychologists' ethical responsibilities conflict with law, regulations, or other governing legal authority, psychologists make known their commitment to the Ethics Code and take steps to resolve the conflict." But the 2002 code created a new enforceable standard: "If the conflict is unresolvable via such means, psychologists may adhere to the requirements of the law, regulations, or other governing legal authority" (Standard 1.02). This new enforceable standard, in my opinion, contradicts one of the essential ethical values voiced in the Nuremberg trials. Even in light of the post-9-11 historical context and challenges, I believe we can never abandon the fundamental ethical value affirmed at Nuremberg. An attempt to modify Standard 1.02 was placed only in the nonenforceable section. In the 5 years since creating this new enforceable ethical standard in a sharp break with the past, APA chose to make no qualifications, restrictions, or other modifications to Standard 1.02 in the code's enforceable section....

Over the decades I've written articles and books examining APA's earliest discussions about ethical responsibilities and accountability, the choice to create an ethics code, the innovative methods used to create a unique code, the revisions and controversies over the years, and APA members' ethical views, dilemmas, and behavior. During the code's distinguished history, it has set forth APA's essential ethics and the standards to which members agree to hold themselves accountable through the Ethics Committee's formal enforcement. For me, the two examples above represent defining issues for APA. Steps that APA has taken or avoided since 9-11 mark a sharp shift in values and direction.

I respectfully disagree with these changes; I am skeptical that they will work as intended; and I believe that they may lead to far-reaching unintended consequences. These changes take APA so far away from its ethical foundation, historic traditions, and basic values, and from my own personal and professional view of our responsibilities, that I cannot support them with my membership. In light of my respectful disagreement with APA about these fundamental changes, it is with great sadness and regret that I resign my membership.

Sincerely,

Kenneth S. Pope, Ph.D., ABPP

Appendix E:
The Mental Health Heresy

by G.C. Dilsaver, P/M, Psy.D, M.T.S.

The following is not a condemnation of those persistent practitioners who have attempted to insert their faith into the mental health paradigm, attempts that if efficacious at all were in spite of that paradigm. Nonetheless, such attempts if uncompromising and orthodox remain on the conceptual level intrinsically impossible, and on the practical level increasingly at odds with the clinical guidelines and ethics of the mental health system.

The attempts to integrate the mental health professions, and clinical psychology in particular, with Christianity have been long spearheaded by the Protestants, and attempted as of late by the Catholics. These attempts have failed. They have failed because such an integration is not possible while preserving an authentic Christian understanding of the nature, or anthropology, of the human person. Indeed, these attempts at so-called "Christian integration" of the mental health professions are rather a subsuming

251

and denaturing of Christian principles unto a dominant mental health paradigm. Indeed, this Christian integration with the mental health professions has resulted in a primary manifestation of today's phenomenon of a compromised, attenuated, and secularized Christianity.

The mental health paradigm is a false one. As the terms "mental" and "behavioral" health indicates, the mental or behavioral health field has reduced that which is considered essential human well-being down to a person's mere mentation and behaviors. But it is not the thoughts or actions of a person that are the sole or even essential concern. Rather it is the heart or soul from which they emanate. But the mental health professions have either nothing to say of this soul; or, if they do, it is diametrically opposed to a true understanding of the Christian understanding. From Freud on, what the mental health field has sought to heal is the *ego*, that is, the *pride* and *self-love* of a person. But this pride and self-love is considered in traditional Christian spirituality an impeding disfigurement of the soul to be purged in the process of sanctification.

Finally, even if the mental health professions give lip-service to the existence of the soul, that soul is nonetheless discounted in the final reductionistic mental health paradigm imposed on all licensed practitioners. According to the DSM and the mental health system a person is but a conglomeration of superficial empirical symptoms, nothing more.

Thus any attempts at Christian integration are doomed to be but window-dressings. So too, such attempts must compromise the Christian understanding of the human person to fit the mental health profession's bottom-line reductionistic view of that person. The true Christian understanding of the human person cannot be subsumed under the mantle of mental health without doing grave harm to that understanding; for the mental health understanding of the human person and its ensuing treatment goals are nothing less than diametrically opposed to that of the traditional Christian understanding. So at best, Christian integration attempts entail a compromise unto heresy, at worst a complete apostasy.

Appendix F:
Training & Certification in Psychomoralitics®

Accreditation

The *Institute of Psychomoralitics* is the only authorized source of training and certification in psychomoralitics. Only certified practitioners (*PCM* or *P/M*) of psychomoralitics may use the term psychomoralitic(s) or claim to practice or use the techniques of psychomoralitics.

Life Experience Prerequisites

All psychomoral clinicians are taken from the proven ranks of life! Whereas the vast majority of psychologists become doctors with the sum total life experience of getting grades while majoring in the narrow field of undergraduate psychology and then continuing to get good grades and jumping through various hoops in graduate school in an even narrower field of clinical psychology, Psychomoral practitioners not only have the academic aptitude shown by a lifelong love of learning but the characterological aptitude to themselves walk-the-walk of human flourishing amidst the travails of existence.

All candidates for Certification in Psychomoralitics have a unique aptitude for empathetic mentoring and understanding and a proven record of living in accord with a holistic application of psychomoralitics (*viz.,www.ImagoDeiWay.com*).

The normal certification process for mentors is two years. Mentors in training must be able to give multiple detailed narrative accounts verbally and in writing of their application of psychomoralitics in personal, familial, or community settings before certification.

Psychomoralitic Prerequisite

All Candidates for Enrollment in the Certification Process must first undergo at minimum one course (7) of psychomoralitic sessions. Continued sessions and supervision as needed is implemented throughout the training process

Common Initial Mentoring Curriculum

Mentoring & Psychomoralitic Tracks follow the same initial four semester (2 year) mentoring curriculum. A student's interest, aptitude, and performance during the coursework determine the track taken.

Psychomoralists

Certified Psychomoralists (*P/M*) are taken from the rank of Psychomoral Certified Mentors (*PCM*) and are qualified to teach psychomoralitics and supervise the training of mentors. Certification as a psychomoralist normally takes an additional 1.5 to 2.5 years (with certification in mentoring; 3 - 4 in total), though conditional certification may be granted prior and time extensions are granted. A Master's Degree in Philosophy or possibly a related field (Theology, Great Books, Literature) or its *informal equivalent* is also required. Psychomoral certification requires the supervision of mentoring casework, the passing of both written and oral exams, the submission of detailed case histories, and a Psychomoralitic thesis.

INSTITUTE OF PSYCHOMORALITICS
Practicing the Soul-Deep Science of Human Flourishing

WWW.PSYCHOMORALITICS.ORG

Psychomoralitics is a ® Registered Trademark.

Abnegation: The receptive subjugation and reduction of the Pseudo-Self, that includes the sequential breaching and reduction of the coping mechanisms, the ego passions, and the ego by impacting reality.

Anxiety: The ego specific manifestation of the passion of fear.

Assent: In the second realm of moral/psychological process the cognitive agreement to a particularization of being as truth.

Avenues of Approach: A pathway exposing the ego to reality created with the chosen breaching of coping and primal defenses.

Character: Distinguished as either tended toward or open to reality or tending away from or closed to reality. Formed by the habituation of the psychomoral act.

Concomitant Passions: In the ego, anxiety is concomitant with fight and/or flight passions. In the psyche, peace is concomitant with joy and/or sorrow.

Coping: The act of successful defensive, denial, or ignoring of certain impacting reality.

Egoistic: Pertaining to the functions of the ego.

Ego: (Lt., *I*) A part of a person, but not an essential part. The ego is in essence an apostatizing pride and subjective self-love. It is the root of both ego-reactivity and mal-being. (In Psychomoralitics, *ego* translates as not only *I*, but as *"me, myself, and I."*)

Ego Defenses: The combination of coping mechanisms and egoistic passions.

Ego-obduracy: The malignant choice to turn away from Supreme Objective Being in a prideful self-love.

Ego-Reactivity: A reaction to anxiety driven fight or flight ego passions.

Emotions: A physiological reaction to the stimuli of impacting reality.

Essential Well-Being: The degree of which depends on the ability to receive-the-real, assent-to-truth, and choose-the-good. This entails the acceptance of ego-abnegation for love of objective truth and good and the subsequent ordering of the ego to the intellect and will and predominance of the psychic passions.

Fight or Flight Passions: A response to anxiety. The summary passion of sadness is a flight passion, whereas anger is a fight passion.

Hyperselectivity: When ego passions cause the coping mechanisms to become frenzied in either an imprudent or irrational manner.

Human Flourishing: A continued and peaceful openness to reality and the full spectrum of human existence from the sublimest joys to the most poignant sorrows.

Mal-Being: The presence of some degree of rational-volitional rebellion against reality, but neither an unawareness, ignoring of, or distortion of that reality.

Maturation: The result of either natural development or psychomoralitic intervention that results in an increased openness to reality and essential well-being.

Mental Health Field: (aka, Behavioral Health, etc.) Comprises all the disciplines and professions that by statutory definition utilize the term "mental health," *et al.*, and as such are controlled in totality by of the mental health system and thus necessarily have the *Diagnostic and Statistical Manual* as a baseline nosology.

Mental Health System: (aka, Behavioral Health, etc.) The controlling entity of all services, practices, and clinical disciplines, that treat "mental health," *et al.* This controlling entity is comprised of and subsidized by the State, the insurance and pharmaceutical industries, and the mental health professions' regulatory and educational agencies.

Mind: The intersect or conjuncture of soul and brain, a grey area of material and immateriality.

Adjoining Passions: The plethora of passions that subsequently accompany those of the chief and summary passions. The passions have been traditionally categorized as love, desire and repugnance, delight and loss, hope and despair, daring and fear, and anger. This list can be expanded by delineating the plethora of "feeling" adjectives both positive and negative.

Chief Passion: The summary and adjoining passions all come from either love of egoistic/subjective good or love of psychic/objective good. Love then is the chief passion, being the *sine qua non* of all the other passions.

Passions: Physical manifestations that have their origins in the impact of reality upon the ego and the psyche. Though the passions have their origins in the psychomoral realm, they can be experienced in the body as physically felt emotions ("emotions" here designating mere physical sensations).

Positive Summary Passions: Glee sums up all the positive ego passions. Joy sums up all the positive psyche passions.

Negative Impacting Reality: That which strikes the ego as abnegation. It strikes the psyche as objective loss.

Negative Summary Passions: Sadness sums up all the negative ego passions. Sorrow sums up all the negative ego passions.

Personality: The overall *presentation* of the person. The more authentic a person is the more the personality ceases to act as veneer but rather both diminishes and manifests a person's character unimpeded by coping mechanisms.

Philosophize: to concentrate our gaze upon the totality of encountered phenomenon and to methodically investigate the coherency of them all and the ultimate meaning of the whole; to examine what "something real" actually is, what man himself is, mind, the complete total of things. (Pieper 1991, 147)

Positive Impacting Reality: That which strikes the ego as gratification. It strikes the psyche as objective gain.

Pseudo-self: The composite of ego, ego passions, and coping mechanisms.

Psyche: (Gk., *soul*) The ultimate perfecting form of that portion of organic matter that together with the psyche (i.e., hylomorphic composition) comprises an individual human being. The human psyche has tripartite faculties. These faculties are categorized, from lowest to highest, as either vegetative, sensitive, or rational. It is from the rational faculties that comes the specific difference of the human person: that of an enfleshed being that has reason and freewill.

Psychomoralitics: is the applied science of the soul that enhances openness to reality and essential well-being by diminishing ego-reactivity and essential mal-being, so as to effect a person's full human flourishing.

Pre-Cognitive: the existential receptivity of reality as being qua being on the intellect before that intellect's cognitive response to it as a specific truth.

Receptivity: An openness to reality that increases to the point of pure receptivity where only the psychic passions are present.

Stagnation: The habitual defending against increasing impacting reality and the maturation and openness it proffers. The resistant therapeutic mode found in coping.

Three Stages of the Psychomoral Act: The first stage is the *existential,* which entails interaction with being as *receiving-the-real.* The second stage is the *cognitive,* which entails interaction with being as an *assenting-to-truth.* The third stage is the *volitional,* which entails interaction with being as a *choosing-the-good.*

> *Receiving-the-Real* is a precognitive and universal encounter with the real as non-particularized being-as-such.

> *Assenting-to-Truth* is a cognitive acceptance of being as a specific or particularized being.

> *Choosing-the-Good* is a volitional embrace of being as the good.

Truth: the cognition of that which exists. Being proclaimed in a particularized manner.

Values: Goods, or objects of the will, that one cherishes.

Vice: Psychomoralitically, egoistic defenses, both coping mechanisms and dominant ego passions, that inure a person from impacting reality.

Virtue: Psychomoralitically, avenues of approach that breach egoistic defenses and open a person up to impacting reality.

Notes:

Notes:

Notes:

CPSIA information can be obtained
at www.ICGtesting.com
Printed in the USA
FSHW021940191218
54590FS